THE SEARCH FOR AWESOME

Ten Experiments in the Quest for Happiness

AMY LOPEZ, PHD

Cover art by Michael Husson.

The Search for Awesome: Ten Experiments in the Quest for Happiness

Table of Contents

Acknowledgments

One of the easiest things we can do to be happy is to be grateful. I am so grateful to everyone who helped and supported me along the way.

Thank you to my family, including my parents, my mother-in-law, my aunt, my siblings, my siblings in-law, and my friends for putting up with me during this time, listening to my theories on happiness, encouraging me, and even joining me in some of my experiments.

I want to thank my happiness book club, who provided me with support, inspiration, and ideas. Thank you for talking me through the tough stuff and being open to trying some of the experiments yourself when I needed feedback. I was honored to have all of you join me on this journey.

I would like to give a special shout out to those who participated in my happy people research. Your stories were a turning point for me. Thank you for sharing them.

I couldn't have done this without my editorial and development team: Toni, Doug, and Maggie at Windword Literary Services, Janet at EmpowerYourAwesomeness.com, and one of my all-time best friends, Michael, who designed the beautiful cover.

I want to thank my spiritual and emotional guidance team: Heather, Matt, Carol, Clarke, Gina, and my MOPS group. Thank you for helping me dig through the crazy to find the hidden gems of truth. I couldn't have done it without you. I want to give a special "thank you" to my guru, Gina, for giving me a safe space to build my cocoon.

Thank you to the congregation of my church for supporting and loving me and for their unusual habit of showing up in strange places when I needed them the most. I also want to thank the staff at my daughter's preschool. Having a safe place for my child is the greatest gift I could have ever received.

Although I know He probably won't be reading this book, I want to express my gratitude to God. In one episode of *The Big Bang Theory*, Mary Cooper says, "When God writes another book, I'll read it." I have come to learn that God has written lots of other books, or at least had a big hand in helping. The same is true for mine.

And most important, I want to thank Mario and Alexandra. Thank you for being the reason. Thank you for being my happy.

Preface

I have always been a pretty happy person. Maybe I shouldn't say that. Anyone who has a childhood nickname "Grouch Lady" probably can't be classified as happy. True, I'm not one of unbridled enthusiasm, but I can say I've had a life well-lived. Like everyone, I've had my struggles, but for the most part, my life has been filled with humor, fun, and happiness. I'd even venture to say it's been awesome.

For the past few years, though, things have been out of whack. Whether I'm having an existential crisis or just getting older, life seems a lot more challenging right now. I think things began to really feel out of control when I got sick. It wasn't a horrible life-threatening illness, but it was pretty uncomfortable. And it was bad timing. This malady came at a time when I was also dealing with a number of other obstacles common in midlife, including becoming a new mom and adjusting to being a parent, completing my graduate studies and trying to figure out my career path, and a job change for my husband that required him to travel several times a month. While he traveled, I was left with my illness, a toddler, uncertainty, and lots of worry and fear. It was more than I could handle. Instead of figuring things out, I fell apart. Completely. I forgot who I was. I forgot how to soothe myself in times of trouble. I forgot how to calm my fears and look for hope. I forgot how to have fun and be happy. In essence, I forgot what made me awesome.

Eventually, my symptoms were managed and my body began to heal, but my soul didn't recover quite so quickly. When I finally started to physically feel better, I decided that letting fear run my brain was no longer acceptable. I wanted to bring back the fun, humor, and joy that had mostly made up my life. I wanted my life to be awesome again. I just wasn't sure how to do it or if it was even possible. I've been a mental health therapist for a long time and have helped many people find their way through dark times, but could I do it for myself? There was only one way to find out. Relying on my clinical and research training,

I took on happiness as a personal pursuit. I read about happiness, tried what the experts recommended, and then wrote it all down. This book is the result of that process.

It wasn't all sunshine and cupcakes—life still happened. I wrestled with both real and imaginary problems. There were times when I wanted to give up. At one point, I didn't even believe that happiness existed. But I kept going, and eventually the project became about more than trying to be happy. It was my attempt to reclaim myself. It was a chance to examine who I was and who I wanted to be. And in the end, I learned some valuable lessons about happiness that I couldn't have found in the happiness experts' research.

This book is not a "How to Be Happy" guide. It doesn't offer suggestions for what will make you happy. It's just one woman's tale of trying to find the humor and hope hidden in the darkness. I hope my story will inspire others to explore their own happiness and to try to create a life they love. Happiness and contentment can be elusive and tricky, but they are attainable. Happiness can be for everyone.

I wish you all peace in your own journeys as you join me on my quest for happiness and my search for awesome.

Chapter 1

The Tragic Backstory

Okay, so maybe that chapter title is a little dramatic, but it sounds a lot more intriguing than "The Rough Patch." Full disclosure: There isn't really anything tragic about my story. Rather, it's just the tale of how I hit a tough time in my life when I lost my happy, which I guess is a little tragic.

I wasn't sure I really wanted to start a book about happiness by talking about misery. However, it seems that most stories that end with happily ever after have the same formula. They seem to all start with some kind of tragedy: Anna and Elsa's parents are killed, Rapunzel gets kidnapped and locked in a tower, a spell is cast on Sleeping Beauty, Cinderella's parents die and she's left in a life of indebted servitude, and Snow White is sent into exile. Yes, it appears that stories that end with happily ever after seem to always start with tragedy.

It's not only fairy tales. I found a similar pattern in the happiness literature. In most of the books I read about happiness, the authors start with some sort of sad story explaining why the author needed to search for happiness. In part, these narratives are a justification and explanation, but I also think these miseries serve as a way to help us all relate to each other. Although our stories may be different, most of us have tales of woe and attempts to avoid suffering. As I read these tales, I frequently found myself nodding in recognition and silently agreeing with their heartache. Their need to change their lives was all too real for me because I needed to change, too. I kept reading because I wanted to know how they did it. I wanted to know that change was possible. I wanted hope for my own transformation.

So, like the other tales that end with happily ever after, (spoiler alert!!) I decided to start my tale with tragedy. I wanted to provide some justification for my quest while also providing some hope to those out there who are searching just like me. My story isn't unique. Rather, there are way too many of us who are living our lives in quiet desperation, wondering where happy went. So, for all you out there trying to navigate your happily ever after, I want you to know you're not alone. I'm guessing that you, too, have a tragic backstory (or a rough patch—call it what you will) that you want to turn into a happy ending. I feel your pain, your desperation, and your fears because they're the same as mine. This isn't just my story, it could be yours, too. You don't have to settle for unhappily ever after. Transformation is possible. Sometimes the pain just has to come first. Maybe my story will encourage you to keep trudging through that rough patch, remembering that happily ever after starts with tragedy. That's just how transformation stories are written.

The Happily-Ever-After Formula

The Charmed Life

I've always been a silly person. Always. My parents will tell you that even as a very young child, I was funny and made them laugh. Throughout my life, humor has been my saving grace, helping me to navigate some pretty tough situations. Until recently, I typically found fun in most things and tried to share this with others. My life was playful and light. I had great friends. I was engaged in meaningful work. I felt like I could make a difference in the world. Life wasn't just happy, it was awesome.

As I reached my mid-thirties, my husband and I realized we were getting older. We decided that if we were going to be parents, we needed to do so before my eggs turned into dust (the doctor's exact words.) I figured, why not? Kids are fun. I would just keep leading a fun life with a new companion by my side. I was not that naive to think that this wouldn't be work, but lots of people have kids and happy lives, right? No big deal.

Wrong. It was a big deal. While I'd known there would be some changes, I didn't realize that once that child arrived, nothing else in the world would matter. Not a single thing. For the first three months of my daughter's life, I was in this beautiful bliss. I didn't care about work or friends or the outside world at all. I was in the process of falling deeply in love. However, when she was about four months old, some of the bliss wore off and reality hit. I went into an ugly postpartum depression. Eventually, I began to feel better, and by the time she was a year old, I was pretty much back to my old self. I even began having fun with parenting. We went to the park, the zoo, and the museum. We spent lazy afternoons in the backyard playing in the sandbox and the baby pool. We watched lots of *Mickey Mouse Clubhouse* and took naps together. In addition, I had consistent child care, so I was able to do some things for me, too. A couple of days a week, I would teach at the university, do volunteer work, or go for a bike ride. This time was quite nice. I was happy.

The Tragedy

Around my daughter's second birthday, I began to not feel great physically. It wasn't anything extreme, just vague symptoms that showed up occasionally. Because I didn't know what was going on, I got scared. I began to have fears about dying and leaving her alone. I regularly worked myself into a panic about what might be going on. I made myself miserable emotionally because I didn't know what was happening physically. The more I worried, the worse it got. Rather than coming up with pretend diagnoses in my brain, I finally decided I would go to the doctor to learn my horrible fate. Turns out, I wasn't dying or going crazy. Rather, I had a fairly common digestive disorder. He prescribed some medication and told me I should be good in a few weeks.

But I wasn't. In part, because I didn't start the medicine like I was instructed. I was too afraid, worried about side effects and "what-ifs."

Instead, I went to a naturopathic doctor, who only made things worse. He fed my fears and persuaded me to try lots of other ways to treat my symptoms. I was so desperate to be healed that I didn't question it. I just accepted that I was in fact really ill and that I was never going to get better without a lot of kale and chakra cleansings and gong vibrations and homeopathy. All this created more chaos in an already confused, fearful, and desperate brain. I probably should have just taken the medication.

Eventually, I went back to my family doctor and confessed all. By then, things had gotten worse. I was in constant pain. My simple illness had progressed to the point where I needed several tests and different treatments to get things under control. To add to my fears, my husband was traveling for work at the time, so not only was I scared, I was alone. I wasn't concerned so much for myself, but what would happen to my daughter if something happened to me? I spent my days living in fear and paralyzed by constant worry. The hardest part was that I didn't know how to comfort myself. All the things I had normally done in the past to survive stress and crisis were no longer available to me. I had lost them to this illness. I couldn't run or do yoga or ride my bike because any exercise at all triggered intense pain. I couldn't get a massage or even give hugs because I couldn't stand to be touched. I definitely couldn't treat myself to a coffee or soothe myself with pizza and ice cream. In fact, I couldn't eat much more than plain bread. All those self-care techniques I had relied on were useless now and I didn't know what else to do. I didn't know how to save myself. I can say that during this time, I was not happy. Not at all.

The Surrender

One night, unable to sleep because of the pain and fear, I decided that I would stop worrying for a few minutes and try to read a book. I perused my bookshelves for something that might take my mind off my problems and came across an old text from one of my college classes. Titled *The Cloister Walk*, it's about a woman who spends a year living at a monastery. There was a line in it that caught my attention: "At the time, I had lost my voice and broken my leg. This was a clear sign from God that I needed to sit down and shut up." I wondered what message

God might be trying to send me. At that moment, I fell to my knees and prayed. It was time to surrender.

Just like tragedy, surrender is a common theme in transformation stories. The statement "I can't do this anymore" is uttered and something magical happens. Transformation stories need surrender to make space for change to happen. For me, surrender meant letting go of trying to control everything and turning it over to God. On that night, I prayed in a way that I hadn't in years. I asked for forgiveness. I asked for help. And suddenly, I no longer felt alone. I knew God was with me. For the first time in several months, I had hope that things just might turn out okay.

Over the next few months, I began attending church, reading Scripture, and praying. All. The. Time. When I felt like I couldn't go on, I prayed. When I was paralyzed by fear, I prayed. When I was in pain and couldn't move, I prayed. I had gotten to the point where praying was all I could do. It provided some relief, especially when I felt like my prayers were being answered. When I prayed because I was feeling alone, the phone would ring. When I prayed because I couldn't handle caring for my child anymore, a neighbor would offer a playdate. When I was afraid of the next medical procedure, the nurse would be wearing a cross around her neck. God reminded me He was there and helped me keep going. By His grace, I survived.

The Quest

While I credit the Lord for pulling me from the pit, I wanted to do more than survive. I was tired of living in fear. I needed to find my awesome buried beneath worry and self-pity. There was too much at stake to just resign myself to a life of quiet misery. Surrender was a start, but there had to be more I could do to make myself feel better. It was time to do more than pray. So I tried. I tried everything I could think of:

- ☺ I completed the Gratitude Project. Every week I wrote a letter to a friend or family member or someone who had helped me. Writing those letters made me realize how many people love and care about me. Gratitude is supposed to be good for the soul. It was for mine.

- ☺ I practiced breathing techniques and relaxation skills, like guided imagery. At those times when I couldn't do anything else, at least I could try to breathe.
- ☺ I went to therapy. I think it helped me to resolve some things, but it was mostly an expensive place to cry.
- ☺ I began to crochet, read fun books, take daily walks, and volunteer at an assisted living facility. These things brought me a lot of momentary peace, and at times, even some joy. Of everything I tried, these things probably helped the most.

Doing these things made me functional. I was no longer completely miserable. I had glimpses of myself. I wasn't crying all the time anymore. I wasn't quite so afraid. I had hope that I could go on. Things were looking up. But I still wanted more. I didn't just want to be functional. I wanted my awesome. I knew there had to be a way to be happy.

I began reading books about happiness. Many of the authors suggest that with some tweaks to our lives, we can make it more enjoyable. These authors indicate that we don't necessarily need to make major life changes, but there are simple things we can do to create a life in which we can find contentment, meaning, peace, and even happiness.

As I read, I began to question these notions. Was happiness really this easy? Would tiny changes actually make that big a difference? Could I quell the quiet desperation inside me and find some contentment just by doing a few things differently? I had to find out.

Just like tragedy and surrender, the quest is an important part of the happily-ever-after stories. I fear that too many of us give up at tragedy or surrender, and I didn't want my story to end like that. I wanted my happily ever after, so I decided to take the journey to rescue my awesome. I would do what these authors suggested as a way to recover my happiness from the monsters of fear and worry. However, since I am a researcher, not a knight or a princess, I decided I'd search for happiness through scientific inquiry and experimentation—a modern-day version of a quest, I suppose.

Happily Ever After?

All the elements of a happily-ever-after story were there: tragedy, surrender, and now the quest. I just needed to take the next step to complete my transformation and arrive at my happily ever after. Because that's just how happily-ever-after stories work. Surely, the same must be true for me, right? Time to find out.

Chapter 2

The Secrets of Happiness

I'm going to start with the results. It's good research protocol to share some findings so that people can decide if they want to read further. However, before I get too far into this, I want to first clarify that this was not really a "research" project. My methods were sloppy, my measures were not validated, I don't cite any of my literature, and there were a number of confounding variables that I'll simply refer to as "life." This is a single-case study and a pilot test. It was less a study and more an "experiment," kind of like a middle school science fair project. And, these aren't really findings so much as observations, which makes me less of a researcher and more of a stand-up comedian. Yeah, that sounds about right.

If you still want to know what happened, despite a lack of scientific rigor, read on.

Question #1: Did it work? Are you any happier?

Answer: Yes, I am happier. However, I can't say for certain why. Just taking on a project like this and the process made me happy. I love having goals and commitments. I love trying something new and seeing it through to the end. In that sense, yes, it made me happier.

From an objective standpoint, my happiness scores increased from start to finish. On the Oxford Happiness Questionnaire, which is my personal favorite happiness scale, I scored a 2.79 at the beginning and a 4.86 at the end. That's a decent increase. In some of the other scales, I didn't notice quite as big a difference. In general, on the other scales, at the start of the project, I was typically in about the 50th percentile, right at the national average. By the end, I was closer to the 60th percentile, indicating that I was happier than about 60% of those who had also completed the happiness scales. Although I had some differences between pre-test and post-test, it's hard to know if there was any true change or if any of the differences were simply the product of my mood on the day I completed the scale. There are so many methodological issues with this design that I'd have to call the results a rough estimate. While I could argue that the answer to the question of whether I'm happier is quantitatively probably "yes," I'm really only comfortable with a strong "maybe."

Although I can't say with any certainty that I am happier, I did learn a lot along the way. I read a lot about happiness. I explored the research about what makes people happy. I understand happiness from many perspectives. While knowing how to be happy and actually being happy are two very different things, I feel confident that I could easily talk someone else through how to be happy or give lectures on what makes people happy. It's just not as easy when I have to do the work myself. Go figure.

Ultimately, what I think any of us who take on a challenge or journey like this learn is that life is not a constant. There are good things and bad things. There are times of sadness and times of joy. There are times of uncertainty and doubt and times of confidence. There are boring times when nothing good or bad is happening. At this moment, I'm happy. Is that a result of my experimentation or just the natural cycle of life? I don't know. While I probably don't have sufficient proof to submit my results to an academic journal, if I were competing in a seventh-grade science fair, the evidence would be good enough to conclude that, yes, my experiments in happiness made me happier. I'll take my blue ribbon now.

Question #2: Did you learn anything that helped you to navigate life better?

Answer: I don't know. I think that's yet to be determined. There were times when I found myself sliding back into self-pity or worry. And despite making a lot of changes in my life that "should" make me happier, it's still very easy for me to get caught up in the day-to-day act of living and all the emotions that come with it. For now, life is pretty quiet, but when the tide turns, I don't know if anything I learned will keep me from falling into the pit of despair. I certainly hope so.

I'd like to think I learned some things that may help others navigate their lives, though. That's the reason I wrote this book. I'm hoping others can learn from my hilarious mistakes. One friend has already told me that she's going to do her own happiness project this year. The possibility that I'm inspiring others to try to reclaim their awesome is one thing that *definitely* makes me happy and provides me hope for the future. I guess we'll see.

Question #3: How can I be happy?

Answer: I don't have any idea. Everyone's path to happiness is different. That's why there is no "secret to happiness." However, if I had to offer a single answer, I'd say live a life that reflects your heart. Do what makes you happy and do less of everything else. You're welcome.

I know that didn't really answer your question. I get it. I wish there was some simple thing I could tell you. Although I don't actually have any answers, I'll share with you some of the things I learned along the way and some tips that might help you find your happy again. By the way, this list isn't exhaustive, and I don't think there's anything on this list that someone else hasn't said before. But, I'll sum it up briefly in case you don't want to read all the way to the end of the book. Again, you're welcome.

1. All the major religions and Bobby McFerrin have it right. Don't worry = be happy. Yep, it really is that easy.
2. Do nothing. Or at least do less. I set out to add in things that would make me happier. But the less I did, the happier I was. Sometimes, all we need to do to find happiness is just be.

3. Go play. It may provide only temporary happiness, but it's a respite from the crazy world. Why do you think kids are so happy?

4. Take the time to figure out what *really* matters. Happiness comes when you prioritize the things you actually care about. Do more of those things.

5. Happiness is easier to find when you're being true to yourself. Don't live someone else's life or get caught up in the shoulds. Happiness is sometimes buried under other people's expectations.

6. Keep good people around you. They can give you support and courage when happiness seems elusive.

7. Sometimes you do have to work at it.

8. Be careful what you wish for. Any time I felt like I needed to practice a happiness skill, the universe obliged my request, and not always in a way that was easy. God has quite the sense of humor.

9. Finding happiness isn't always happy. Growing can be hard. Changing can be hard. At times, finding happiness was more painful than I expected it to be.

10. Sometimes, happiness is bigger than just us. I didn't realize how much of a spiritual journey this was going to be. This quest wasn't just about finding my awesome, it was about renewing my faith and strengthening my relationship with God. When I live the life God intended for me and trust that the plan He has for us is good, happiness was a lot easier to find.

Question #4: The list above seems like a lot of work. Can you just give me one single thing I can do to make me happier right now?

Answer: Yes. Be around other people.

At one point in my quest, I was ready to give up. I didn't believe happiness existed, but I wasn't sure. So I started asking other people. Turns out there are people who do love life. There are people who are happy. And among all these happy people, there was one commonality: their relationships. Every single happy person said good relationships with friends and family contributed to their happiness. Every single person. I don't think that's a coincidence.

All the current happiness research supports this. More than any other factor, the quality of interpersonal relationships is the strongest predictor of happiness. If you want to be happy, engage in human relationships. Have genuine conversation. Hug. Laugh. Reach out to others. Be completely present. Be happy together. Once again, you're welcome.

As promised, the secrets of happiness summed up. But, there is likely a little more to it. So keep reading. You may find some insights, some humor and maybe even a secret gem that I didn't list here. Thanks for joining me on this journey. I hope my story will bring some happiness to your day.

Chapter 3

The Quest Begins

Glad you're still with me. This is where things get good!

By mid-December of 2015, I had pretty much decided that being happy would be my 2016 resolution. By January 2017, I would be a happier person. Or at least I was going to try. I just wasn't sure how was I going to make it happen. Like all good researchers do, I started by going to the literature for a guide. I looked for books about people who had transformed their tragedies into hope, and I found several. However, I couldn't really travel to Italy, India, and Indonesia like Elizabeth Gilbert did. I couldn't go hike the Pacific Crest Trail like Cheryl Strayed. And I certainly couldn't go find myself a billionaire playboy like E.L. James' book suggests (I know it's not really the same genre as the other stories—just an idea I *briefly* considered). No, I needed a way to find my happy that wouldn't blow my budget or require me to take time away from my job and my child. I had to find happiness right where I was.

After a thorough search of the literature around happiness, I decided that Gretchen Rubin's *The Happiness Project* was a good model. In her book, she takes on several small projects in her home, with her family, or in her career, all designed to increase her overall happiness. It was simple, straightforward, and provided me with a chance to explore many areas of my life. I made some modifications based on my time frames and to fit my personality style, but it seemed easy enough.[1] All I needed to do was try a bunch of things over the course of the year and hope for the best.

Here was my plan:

1. Find different areas of happiness with which I could experiment. Based on current literature, I selected ten things that the research indicated would make people happier. I read studies on each subject area and set up small experiments to try some things out to see if I was any happier after doing them. I called these my "areas of inquiry" to make me sound smart.

2. Set up a blog so I could record my progress.

3. Get a group of people to go on the quest with me.

Areas of Inquiry

Step one was pretty simple. Based on the research and my own past experiences, I made a list of the various areas of my life that might affect my happiness and the experiments I could conduct. Just thinking about these things gave me hope and some happiness. I hadn't even actually started this journey yet and was already making progress. Yay, me!

I intended to try a new experiment each month, but it didn't work out that way. There were some months when I just couldn't take on anything new (sorry, July). There were some months when I needed to repeat a previous experiment because something happened that impacted that area of happiness. There were also times when issues or problems arose and I had to deal with those areas of inquiry sooner than expected. I couldn't realistically say, "That's April's experiment, so I won't worry about it until then." In a way, I ended up having all ten experiments going at the same time. So rather than stopping and

---

1 A note to Gretchen Rubin's lawyers: On Facebook she posted, "What advice would you give to someone who wants to do their own happiness project?" I responded, "Keep a blog so you can write your own book. That's what I'm doing." She liked my comment, so I'm taking that as permission to use her idea. I'm pretty sure a Facebook like is the same thing as a binding legal contract.

starting at the beginning of each month, the experiments became a work in progress, with new sets of skills building on each other.

For each of the experiments, I designated a "happiness quotient." This was my own arbitrary rating system of how much that area affected my overall happiness. The happiness quotient doesn't really mean anything—it's just a quick reference for those of us who like to think in numbers. It provides a basis for comparison among the areas. And it makes me sound more scientific and mathematical (and smart). The happiness quotient is actually just a trick to make everyone think this was a serious study. Happens in research all the time.

Writing it Down

Next, I set up a blog. I made an agreement with myself to write at least once a week so I could track my progress. As it turned out, writing was a lot more fun than I'd expected, so I wrote more than weekly. Sometimes I wrote every day. It was a place for me to record my plans and ideas, what I had done, what I hadn't done, and whether I was any happier based on that month's work. The regular act of writing, organizing my thoughts, and keeping track of my happiness also contributed to my happiness. It was quite enjoyable! Thinking about what I was going to do and setting up the blog had given me hope. I still hadn't officially started any of the experiments and I was already happier! This was going to be easier than I'd thought!

The Group

My final step was to find a group of people to join me. I figured it would not only give me support and encouragement along the way, but could also help generalize any findings. Larger sample sizes are always better when applying research to the general public. I invited family, friends, and community members to join me in my experimentation with happiness.

When I made the invitation, I was overwhelmed by how many responses I got to my request. About twenty people from around the country and from all areas of my life said they were interested. We agreed to set up meetings in person and via Skype. I created an interactive page where people could post their thoughts and progress. It was very exciting to me that there were so many others also interested in happiness. It made me happy that I could help others be happy.

Ultimately, though, life got in the way of the group. We had two meetings and a few online discussions, but by February the group had pretty much fizzled out. I kept the page going, as many wanted to follow my progress, but I quickly realized I was a lone wolf. This was no longer a group design; I was back to a single-case study. The people from my group remained my biggest supporters, though, and some of them are planning to try again—someday. For now, let's just say the group is "in progress."

Happy People Survey

Although not part of my original plan, I added in the Happy People survey as a fourth step to my project. At one point, I became pretty disheartened. I felt like happiness just wasn't possible—for me or for anyone else. In all the books I was reading, there were lots of suggestions on how to be happy but very few stories that depicted what a happy person looks like or revealed what happens once the journey is over. They reach happily ever after, but then what? When people make changes, does it stick? Do people stay happy? Or do they get sucked back into the routine of life once they stop paying attention to their happiness? The books didn't say.

Maybe it was my worldview at the time, but it seemed to me that everyone was unhappy. As I looked around in the media, among my friends, family, co-workers, and community, I couldn't come up with even a single example of someone who loved his or her life, let alone someone who was extraordinarily happy. Was there anyone in the world who wasn't overwhelmed by the very process of existence?

I set out to find an example of a happy person. I asked quite a few people if they were happy and, if so, why (so that I could do the same thing). While I did find a lot of people who were also stuck in the same quiet desperation I was, I also found quite a few happy people. There were more happy people than I expected, and the responses they gave me as to what made them happy were very interesting, maybe even more interesting than my project. Although I originally set out to find happiness only within myself and the ten areas of inquiry, this little diversion from my path provided me with very valuable information. Let's just call this my "bonus experiment."

Helping Others

My final step is still in progress. At the end of the project, I began talking about my experience and was surprised by the response. People were interested, curious. I got a lot of questions about how others could take on this type of project and start examining their own happiness. I realized that there may be something valuable in all I've learned and experienced.

The Happy People survey provided me a lot of insight into what we can do both as individuals and as a community to create a happier place. In fact, I've become so interested in what makes people happy that I plan to continue seeking out more people to find out about the lived experience of happiness. I don't believe my work is done. Talking about happiness has become my passion, my purpose, and my reason to get out of bed. I've come to realize how incredibly important happiness is to human existence, and I can't keep this to myself. I don't know where this will take me, but I can't wait to find out. This book is where it began, but I hope it will continue. I'm pretty sure *this* is my happily ever after.

Making Space

Area of Inquiry: Get my home and life organized

Methods:

- Clean out my house
- Complete necessary construction projects
- Get help cleaning up

Happiness Quotient: 5/10

Experiment Design:

Getting organized seemed like a good place to start. Before undertaking any project, what do most people do? They get themselves organized. They create a space to work. They make sure they have all the things necessary to complete the project. In fact, everyone in my book club also chose getting organized as a January goal. Makes sense. We need to clean up after the holidays and prepare for the coming year. Time to get rid of the old to make room for the new. Although I wasn't sure if it would make me happier, I focused on this area first as a way to get my mind, my space, and my emotions ready for the work that was to come.

The literature around cleaning and organizing is mixed. It's not really related to the happiness literature, but there are a number of books that talk about how having an organized space is typically good to help us focus and bring about calm. That's the whole point of feng shui right? Despite the lack of grounded literature, I still decided that I would give it a go. Cleaning my house had to be done anyway, may as well combine it with my happiness project.

Getting my house organized seemed like an easy experiment to begin with. The physical work of organizing my house was also a lot less frightening than taking on the emotional toll of dealing with parenting or relationships. Throwing out a bunch of broken crap and organizing my closets seemed like a manageable, emotionless task. In analytic psychology, the house is representative of the self. It's possible that I chose this experiment subconsciously because both my house and my soul needed a good scrubbing. Either way, something was going to get cleaned with the hope that I could find happiness buried in the clutter

Get My Space Organized

My house is more than my living space and where I spend my time, it's my place of refuge and my peace. However, it is very easy for my home to be taken over by too much stuff and too little space. When I took on this project, cleaning my house really needed to be done. I felt a little like my house was closing in on me. Something needed to change, quickly.

While my house is rarely messy, at this point in my life, it was bursting at the seams. My table was filled with papers, mail, and all the junk that I empty out of my purse. My closets were filled with clothes I will never use. I really doubt that I will have any need for my high school prom dress or three denim vests awaiting the day when denim vests might make a comeback. In addition to my vintage clothing, my closets were also filled with lots of other really unimportant stuff: games with missing pieces, elementary school art projects, notes from my undergraduate classes, and half-completed art projects from times when I'd thought myself to be "crafty."

While my own stuff was easily tossed out, I was on the fence about what to do with all the baby items. I couldn't toss out the outfit my daughter wore home from the hospital. Or her first Valentine's Day dress. Or the really cute one she wore on a random Tuesday afternoon. I'm pretty sure there are no more babies coming, but I felt a little sad thinking about just letting it all go. Maybe I don't have to get rid of all the baby clothes and toys just yet…

By January 2, I'd gotten rid of three trash bags, donated two boxes of stuff, and even managed to give away some of the baby toys. It felt like a good start. Things felt more organized and somewhat lighter. Had I found happiness yet? Had it been buried under the Halloween decorations and the unused camping equipment?

Nope. In fact, I was already being hard on myself for not having done more. I had to remind myself that this was a yearlong process and I didn't have to get all of it done immediately. I reminded myself that it's okay to slow down and breathe. This was a work in progress. I guess I'd been hoping for a quick and easy answer to being happier. Yet, I didn't find my awesome buried among the junk mail. If only it were that easy.

After that first week, I fizzled out completely. I'd had the best of intentions, but life got in the way. I had to return to work, the weather was crappy, my husband was traveling for work, and my daughter was readjusting to being back at school. I was tired, and the last thing I wanted to do was clean and organize. I was only two weeks into my project and already I'd lost my spark and given up. Maybe happiness wasn't worth all this work.

But it was only January, too soon to give up. So I just slowed down. I gave myself some space to search for happiness while still living life. Putting more pressure on myself obviously wasn't going to make me happy. Instead of working so hard, I did less. I took on my house a little at a time. I made an organizational plan that balanced my housekeeping with my other responsibilities. Every week, I would first focus on necessary tasks (dishes, laundry) and then spend a little extra time in one room each day. For the most part, this worked well and helped me stay on top of the messes before they could become too big and overwhelming. I gave myself some breaks in between to just admire all the work I'd already done. Sometimes I'd just sit in a clean room and look at it. Maybe it was the feeling of accomplishment or just being in a clean and quiet place, but this act of just being after cleaning made me feel happy. Somehow, doing less work and relaxing in the presence of my small accomplishments made me happier than pushing myself to get it done. Who knew?

Cleaning was a practical task, but interestingly, it also provided me the opportunity for some contemplation. One afternoon while cleaning my daughter's room, I was trying to put some games away on the top shelf of the closet under all her puzzles, when I got a little lazy. I can just slip them under, I thought. *No reason for the extra step of moving the puzzles first.* Within moments, I was precariously balancing the games in one hand while trying to shield myself from the puzzle pieces raining on my head. So much for shortcuts. Luckily, it ended up being only a few puzzles that I had to put together, but I lost a piece in the process. But I didn't worry about it. One of the things I've learned in my few short years of parenting is that those lost puzzle pieces always seem to show up eventually. I was right and the missing piece showed up a few weeks later.

I know that this story in itself really isn't very interesting. It doesn't have that much to do with happiness (or really anything at all). I don't think it's even a story I'd bother repeating to anyone. Even if I spruce up the details some, it's only slightly interesting. But it made me philosophical. I remember as a young social work intern listening to an older therapist talk about the despair of one of his clients. I made the naïvely hopeful comment, "But things always fall into place eventually." Although this was probably twenty years ago, I'll never forget his response: "Yes, until they fall out of place again." He wasn't being cynical, just giving me my first lesson in the nature of impermanence.

Putting away the games was a metaphor for my life. I try to precariously balance things. I take shortcuts and things fall. I pick up the pieces and put the puzzle back together. Sometimes, pieces get lost in the process, but I usually find them again. The simple act of cleaning up my daughter's room brought me some hope with the simple reminder about how things change. Maybe my missing awesome would eventually turn up, too.

The Housekeeper

One of my other goals for January was to get some help with cleaning and organizing. I knew that neither my husband nor my child was going to be any help in this process. My mother-in-law had been suggesting for years that I hire a housekeeper. She really thought it would take a big burden off me if there were someone to take care of the things that I didn't have time for, like cleaning the bathtub, dusting, and deep-cleaning the floors. Simple, right? Nothing is ever simple for me.

A few years back, when my husband and I were both working a lot and had some extra money, I had someone come every other week to clean. It was awesome and difficult at the same time. The day before the housekeeper came, I had to do a fair amount of cleaning myself. I know that sounds ridiculous, but anyone who's used a housekeeper knows what I'm talking about. Although the housekeeper does the down and dirty work of the scrubbing, you have to make things clean enough for her to scrub. The dishes have to be out of the sink. The toiletry items have to be put away. The clothes can't be left on the floor. It's a lot of work. In fact, having someone come clean my house was sometimes a source of more stress than happiness. My husband would frequently question me, saying "Who cleans before the housekeeper comes?" "Everyone," I'd reply. I don't think he believed me.

Despite the extra work I knew it would mean for me, I finally gave in to my mother-in-law and hired someone. My decision was precipitated by my not wanting to mop the floor when we were expecting company. So I hired someone, and she did a good enough job of mopping that I ended up having her come regularly. It wasn't like she did anything I couldn't have done myself—it was just nice to have someone else to do it. The work I did to prepare for her was stuff I needed to do anyway. It made my house look better, which made me feel better. In the end, doing less of the cleaning did free up some time for other things, and my mother-in-law no longer commented about it, which made me *really* happy.

The Remodel

If you're a contractor or love one, I apologize in advance, but contractors are awful. Really, they're horrible, awful people. I know I shouldn't say that. As individuals, I'm sure they're lovely. But as a whole, contractors are the worst. Really.

A little context. We've lived in our house for nearly twenty years, and in that time, we've done nothing to the house beyond maintenance and minor improvements, so it was a pretty big deal when we decided to remodel our bathroom. I was super-excited, as our old one was this ugly blue with tile that had fireworks on it. After the remodel, the bathroom looked a lot better, but the contractor had taken quite a few shortcuts, which resulted in some problems. Among them was a crack in our bathtub. Trying to get the contractor to take responsibility for his error and then getting it subsequently fixed was really difficult. It had worn me out and the last thing I wanted to do was deal with another contractor. Ever. But, I had to. About a year after that, we had some problems with other plumbing in the house. I found a new contractor, but he also did a less-than-adequate job and then tried to persuade us to work with a "friend" of his to clean up some of the mess he'd made. And then there was the contractor I hired to replace my exterior doors. He had great reviews, but he let his apprentice do most of the work, and it looks like an apprentice did the work. The trim doesn't match up, and the doors let light and air in. I had to hire someone else to come and fix that one, too. I wonder if contractors stay in business by just going around correcting each other's mistakes. Anyway, yeah, contractors are awful.

Fast-forward to my happiness experiment. One aspect of the plan to organize my house was to finish up these lingering unfinished remodel projects. They'd been a source of unhappiness for me for a while, so they needed to get done. These projects were just a mess, but I was too exhausted to deal with it. After everything else I have been through in the past few years, I just didn't have the energy to find a non-awful contractor. But we couldn't wait any longer. My happiness depended on it.

I'd been looking for a contractor for over a year. I signed up for contractor referral websites, asked for referrals on my neighborhood Facebook page, and asked anyone I met if they knew of anyone who could do the job. I even hung out in front of the local hardware store in hopes of bumping into someone who seemed promising. But as both the manager at Home Depot and a very understanding vice cop explained to me, it's inappropriate to ask strangers if they would be willing to come back to my house to check out my plumbing. Despite all my hard work, I still didn't have a contractor. I was considering just doing the work myself. Me, some YouTube videos, and a power drill—what could go wrong?

Then, from out of the blue, someone posted on our neighborhood website that he was starting a new home remodel business and was looking for some small projects. I contacted him, and he turned out not to be awful. In fact, he turned out to be awesome. By the end of the summer, the work was done and looked great. This made me very, very happy.

The process of the remodel hadn't made me happy. It took much longer than expected and cost more than we'd anticipated, and it's just a little weird to have someone else in your home for several weeks, regardless of how awesome they are. But it had to be done; I'd been ignoring the problem for way too long. It was a huge relief to address this lingering issue and be able to cross this off my list. Although now I have a whole new list of projects for him.

Findings and Analysis

While not life-changing, organizing and cleaning were a good start. Overall, I was able to keep things relatively organized, which brought me some peace of mind. I was even able to get rid of the baby clothes by giving them to a co-worker who was expecting. I did keep a box of my favorite outfits, though. I also kept the baby carrier, just in case. Who knows, maybe I'll be one of those ladies who carry around small puppies or cats in carriers. Or I might use it to carry a hot water bottle to keep my chest warm at sporting events. Or groceries when I want to text while shopping. Or another baby. The possibilities are really endless.

Along the way to getting more organized, I found a number of similarities between cleaning up and happiness. For example, I found that when I dealt with things instead of letting them pile up, they were easier to handle. Just like doing laundry regularly, we have to pay attention to problems and emotions before all the bad stuff becomes too overwhelming. Both cleaning and life problems have to be dealt with on a regular basis, not just when we can no longer stand looking at the mess.

I also found that the peace of mind that cleaning up brought me was temporary. It wasn't long before I had to do it all again. I think happiness works the same way. We just assume that once we find it, we're done, but just like a clean house, happiness isn't permanent. Things change. Things need to be upgraded. Things need to be thrown out. In my moments of unhappiness, I've learned to remind myself that I can get rid of things that are no longer needed in my life, just like my denim vests. Then I have room for the good stuff to come in (including whatever the current fashion version of a denim vest is.)

In my final metaphor, I found that in both organizing and finding happiness, we have to make some decisions about what to keep and what to let go. We may have to deal with things that have been ignored. We may have to ask for help if we can't do it with just a power drill and YouTube. We have to be vigilant about not returning to old habits, instead doing our best to protect that space once it's been cleaned up.

Although my goals were to clean out the closet, I think I cleaned out my brain a bit, too. Doing this experiment prepared me to take on the rest of my happiness experiments. Cleaning out the closets and sorting through all my stuff served as practice for figuring out what's important, for deciding what I want to keep and what I need to get rid of. I know there are plenty of things in my life that are no longer serving me, and maybe it's time to let them go. I wonder if Goodwill accepts fears and regrets?

Chapter 5

The Meaning of Life

Area of Inquiry: Spirituality

Methods:

- Explore the mysteries of the universe
- Better understand my own belief system
- Learn the Bible
- Get more involved with the church
- Strengthen my relationship with God

Happiness Quotient: 9/10

Experiment Design:

Seems like an extreme title, but since I went small for my first experiment, I decided to go really big for my second one. I recognize that spirituality is a vague, poorly defined concept, but I wanted to be able to explore all aspects of human existence outside our own egos. Okay, maybe that's too big, but I'm ready for it.

What does spirituality have to do with happiness? The research indicates that people who have a spiritual life tend to be happier. However, the reasons are mixed. For some, happiness comes from feeling connected to something bigger, something that provides a sense of purpose. For some, being around other believers provides a community and a natural support system. For others, it's not religion but the beliefs, rituals, and resources that provide comfort by providing a way for people to let go of their worries. Casting cares to a higher power or asking the universe or God or angels to help can provide solace and comfort. Believers often find hope in difficult situations. If things don't go as planned, people can find reassurance and resilience in believing that everything happens for a purpose, that it's part of a divine plan, or that something even better is coming. Spiritual people are happier people for lots of different reasons.

However, these beliefs can also come with a cost, especially when formalized religion is involved. While attending religious services can serve as a protective factor against loneliness and depression, for some, religion can also be a great source of guilt, obligation, and fear. These things then negate the happiness benefits. In recent years, Americans have been moving away from formalized religion but still consider themselves to be spiritual. They want the hope, just not the doctrine or judgment. Given all these complicating factors, it's hard to discern exactly what it is about religion that makes people happy (or unhappy, as the case may be.) Is the relationship between spirituality and happiness rooted in ritual? Or does it exist because spirituality provides some guidance about dealing with worry? Are people happier because they have a community? Does spirituality provide an identity that can help people better understand what makes them happy? Is it all of these things? Is it none of them and I'm way off track? Is what all the televangelists say true and God's grace is all we need to be happy? I probably couldn't answer all my questions through my experiment, but I figured they would provide me a place to start and give me a chance to sort through what I personally believe, the role spirituality plays in my life, and how these beliefs may influence my attempts to be happy.

Religious History

Over my life, I've had a mixed relationship with the concepts of spirituality and religion. As a child, I went to an easygoing Protestant church. I did the Christmas plays and sang the songs. I felt loved and connected to the congregation. I hadn't yet developed the capacity for abstract thought, but I enjoyed the music, the snacks, and the friendships our family formed through the church. As I moved into adolescence and developed both the ability for abstract thought and a bit of a rebellious streak, I found that I couldn't just sit through Sunday school or sermons quietly. I had too many questions about the rules and apparent contradictions. I began to explore the Bible beyond the comforting children's stories and found it to be confusing. And I definitely didn't like seeing people be persecuted or discriminated against in the name of God. It didn't make sense. I began to pull away from formalized religion. I still believed in God, but I had a lot of unanswered questions. I found that I could connect to God while sitting on a chair lift better than I could while sitting in a church pew, so the ski area became my Sunday morning chapel.

When I went to college, I was introduced to Catholicism. I was both struck by its beauty and overwhelmed by its rules. I lived with people who understood faith in a completely different way. I met people who gave up their entire lives to serve God. I encountered people for whom the church was all they had, and it was enough. I met people who lived their lives in complete reliance on the Lord. I was astounded by the level of commitment to both their faith and the church. Although I never truly understood the doctrine or rituals, I admired the way the priests, nuns, and other believers took their responsibility to God so seriously, living a life in service to Christ. I came to learn that there were many different ways to express faith. I began to see how the relationship with God was about more than religious services, prayers, or reading the Bible. Rather, I witnessed and experienced how serving and caring for others was service to God.

Although I never really reconnected with a church after college, these experiences helped me to develop a strong spiritual life. I relied on

God for guidance and I could see examples of the Holy Spirit working around me and within me. I served God by serving others. I ended up becoming a social worker, something I have always believed to be a divine calling. While I believed in God, I believed in other things, too. I believed in angels. I believed in reincarnation. I believed in karma and the power of the universe. I believed in tarot, astrology, and psychic energies. I talked to dead relatives and believed they sent me messages. I found God during hikes, and yoga, and in the laughs of babies. I studied Judaism and Buddhism and learned to use tarot cards. Believing in all of this at the same time never felt contradictory to me. In fact, it felt very whole, very complete. I felt supported by the universe and God, regardless of what anyone called it.

Then something changed. I can't tell you what, because I don't really know. For whatever reason, I no longer believed in anything. I could not find connection to the universe through church, or Jesus, or angels, or spirit guides, or psychic revelations. I didn't even really know what I believed. And then it went beyond disinterest and turned into anger. But again, I couldn't tell you why. One day, while perusing Netflix, we came across the *Veggie Tales* shows, in which the characters read Bible verses and sing songs about God's love. My daughter adored it and would walk around the house singing "Trust in God." For some unknown reason, this really pissed me off. Why was I so angry about God's love? I had no idea. I wondered if there was a chance that God was using some of those annoying songs to get my attention. God would need to try harder than a singing cucumber to get me to take notice.

Then I got sick. That definitely got my attention. I wish now I would have just listened to that cucumber. Instead of a gentle reminder, I ended up with a kick in the gut as a wakeup call for me to get my s%#* together. So I did. Or I tried anyway. In the depths of my pain, I had no choice but to pray. I didn't know if it would work, but I had to start somewhere. I asked God for help. I asked for forgiveness. I asked to come home like the prodigal son. With each prayer, I found some solace, some peace, some hope. And I began to believe again. But while prayer was a good start, I thought I needed to do more. I began attending church, reading the Scriptures, doing daily devotionals, and reassessing what it is I believe. Through this process, I learned a little more about God's love.

However, I also found fear. What if my illness was a punishment for being rebellious? God had destroyed the entire world with a flood, sent droughts and famines, and brought all kinds of wrath upon nonbelievers and evildoers. At least that's what the Bible said. Although I don't know that my disbelief and doubts fell into the same categories as murder and enslavement, I didn't want to take any chances. Having to deal with a locust infestation was the last thing I needed. Just to be safe, I figured I'd better not believe in anything but God. I didn't even want to toy with the idea of reincarnation or ghosts or anything other than the Holy Spirit, for fear of dishonoring a vengeful God. I even stopped reading my horoscope, just in case.

I tried to be pious, follow all the rules, and avoid sin and temptation as best I could. I prayed. I believed. But it was hard work. I couldn't live my whole life trying to please an angry deity. I was already afraid of lots of other things, I couldn't be scared of God, too. I really wanted to believe in a loving God, the God of my childhood church. But I couldn't find him in my books, devotionals, or in the church sermons. Where was He?

I didn't know, so I brought in help. I needed to better understand how Christians navigate this dichotomy of a loving God who allows (or causes) really bad things to happen. I went to Bible study. I talked to pastors. I read books about Christianity. The words of Thomas Merton, Henri Nouwen, and C.S. Lewis provided explanations and different perspectives on God's love during difficult times. I also tried to have a little fun with it. My favorite read in this whole process was *Lamb: The Gospel According to Biff, Christ's Childhood Pal.* Not only did this book teach me a fair amount about the Bible, it reminded me that God has a sense of humor.

Although my focus was on Christianity, I wanted to understand the perspectives of faith from different lenses. As I became less afraid of angering a vengeful God, I felt confident enough to explore other religions and belief systems, too. I wanted to know what everyone said. I read several different religious books and found the writings comforting and beautiful. They weren't at all contradictory with what Jesus said. In fact, they all kind of say the same things. From what I could glean, pretty much every religion says, "Don't worry, be kind to others, and recognize that everyone has times in life when things are good and times when things are bad." While there are many things about the universe that I still don't understand, through some of this work, I was able to accept that human struggle is probably not necessarily wrath or vengeance or karma. Life just sucks sometimes. Spirituality is about figuring out how to get through it.

Reading, talking to others, and learning more about religion helped me have a better sense of what I believe and why. It allowed me to understand and experience God's love and grace. But there seemed to be one thing that was still getting in the way: The Bible.

The B-I-B-L-E: Is That the Book for Me?

The Bible has been named the most important and influential book of all time, and it's certainly a top seller. It's been translated into almost every language and can be found throughout the world. The Bible is the foundation for all Christian religious practices, and some believe it to be the direct word of God. Even scientists and philosophical thinkers suggest reading it because of its historical, political, and cultural relevance. If I was going to explore my beliefs, I thought, it was probably important to know what the Bible *actually* has to say. I want to be a believer, but I don't want to just believe what others tell me. That kind of thinking has caused too many problems in our world. Rather, I figured I would find out for myself.

A quick aside: I'm going to sound a little ignorant here, but before I started reading the Bible, I never realized how many elements of today's culture are directly from the Bible. Sayings, ideas, phrases, metaphors, song lyrics—all right from the Bible. Each time I came across a phrase or story in the Bible and recognized it from somewhere else, I was a little surprised. I wonder if others realize how much of our popular culture comes directly from Christian roots.

Anyway, as for the Bible itself, all I can say is, what a mess. I say that with the most love and respect imaginable. As anyone who has read the entire Bible can attest, this is one crazy book! It's filled with wrath, destruction, evil, violence, anger, envy, murder, sex, slavery, famine, and drought. There are also oh so many rules. There are guidelines for what to do if a pregnant woman gets punched during the course of a fist fight and how to handle a wayward bull that goes around goring everyone. I think Leviticus was probably written by the Centers for Disease Control of the time, as it's mostly about managing mildew and pus. There are lots of instructions on how to build things and at times, the Bible reads like an Ikea instruction manual. You'll also find plenty of lists of who "begat" whom, but then they sometimes sell those same relatives into slavery, or take their wives, or murder them or other such things.

In addition to all this craziness, there's a lot of really bad stuff, too. They call it the Good Book, but I often find it to be more of a horror novel. It's a scary book with numerous examples of utter obliteration and annihilation, especially when people don't heed warnings to repent. There are lots of times when God is not kind but, in fact, quite mean. I skipped over most of the prophets because their predictions are just too violent for me. What if God really is this angry?

But while there's the death and destruction, there's a lot of good stuff in there, too. There are stories of love, compassion, hope, and peace. There are promises of redemption, rescue, and salvation. At times, the Bible is as soothing as it is scary. The Psalms offer a way to rejoice and find comfort. Even the violent prophets ultimately find a way to offer hope. The New Testament reminds us that Jesus was sent as a way to avoid all this wrath and destruction. He reminds us of what is good. Jesus takes away some of the fear and acts as the balm that makes the sting of the wrath bearable—mostly. Although Jesus preaches love, forgiveness, and peace, he has some scary warnings, too. Some of his parables include admonitions, with talk of gnashing of the teeth and burning up in the "fiery furnace."

Over the past year, I'd been so fearful of things beyond my control that the last thing I needed was to add a vengeful and hypersensitive God into the mix. In conversation with several pastors, I brought up my concerns about an angry God. They offered a lot of advice, and among the best was that I shouldn't take things so literally. They helped me understand how the Bible was put together in context of the political climate of the time. I stopped trying to read the Bible as an instruction manual but rather as a political thriller, like a 500 B.C. David Baldacci book. I came to see that much of the scary stuff in the Bible was a stab at the ruling class and a call for social justice. A lot of what I believed to be God's wrath was probably just human conflict, but attributing wrath and destruction to a higher power was a great way to get people to conform. Still is.

Ultimately, I was able to see the Bible as more than just a way to scare me into compliance. It's a compilation of man's struggles, through good times and bad. It's the story of humans and their attempts to make sense of a world that often doesn't make any sense. Through the help of many people, I'm better able to see the Bible for what it is: a book full of love, kindness, forgiveness, grace, and faith, with lots of political subtext, exaggeration, intrigue, and human foibles mixed in. While I was able to find some hope in the Scriptures, I don't know that reading the Bible necessarily made me happier. Reading and knowing the Bible has strengthened me spiritually and intellectually. I have a better sense of what I believe, how my beliefs diverge from tradition, and why I believe what I do. I also have the knowledge to understand and challenge others who might try to use God's name to justify bad behavior. While it didn't necessarily make me happier per se, this part of the experiment provided me a nice reminder of what a little knowledge and understanding can do.

Organized Religion

One of the other ways I attempted to understand spirituality was through my involvement with a religious organization.[2] I thought it

2 I want to clarify that I did not really explore *religion*. I did some readings about other religions, but the focus of my experiment was Christianity. I guess even I am so entrenched in Christian privilege that I use the words *religion* and *Christianity* interchangeably. I realize that this is not correct and that I make a lot of generalizations about religion that really apply only to Christianity. I'm sorry for that. Just accept my apology—the last thing I need is more religious guilt.

would be a good place to find a community and learn more about God. I hoped it would help provide me a place to serve. I wondered if the weekly sermons and lessons would help me find hope. I wanted to see if going back to church would make me happy.

When I decided to return to church, I had a great plan. Each week, I would try out a different church, sit in the back, observe, and decide which one to join after several services. I guess God had other plans. I started with a small Presbyterian church a few blocks from my house. The moment I walked in, I knew it was the place for me. The service was exactly like the one at my church from childhood. I could only think, "I'm home." So much for my plan, God made my decision for me.

I began attending regularly and found a community. There were no other young people like me, but within the first few weeks I had an adopted grandmother and had met quite a few people who had a lot of interesting stories to share. I heard a lot of good messages, too. In fact, I often wondered if the pastor sneaked into my home during the week and read my journal, as so much of what he said applied directly to me. I began to look forward to going every week, eager to spend time with my community and figure out how to apply the lessons to my life. In addition to attending worship, I engaged with people at fellowship events and helped out on service projects.

While the research is clear that spirituality can make people happy, religion can get in the way of that. There are rules and expectations. When you're part of a community, you're expected to participate in that community. I took that perceived obligation to heart. Like anything else, it started out with a few minor requests. Since I had a child, it was strongly suggested that I help out with Sunday school. But somehow, it escalated from preparing a lesson every six weeks to being responsible for the entire program. Then I ended up on some committees. I somehow got elected as an elder without my knowledge. Then I was building the church's website. And planning an Easter egg hunt. And organizing a Bible study. Yes, I'd asked God to help me find a community and a place to serve, but this was a little much. I couldn't do it all, but I felt really guilty saying no, so I did all that was asked. Isn't that what good churchgoers do? I spent a lot of time stressed out about it while also feeling guilty for not wanting to do it. What had been a source of comfort and happiness was now making me quite unhappy. I understood why the literature around religion and happiness is mixed. Between the rules of a vengeful God in the Bible and the expectations of a polite yet pushy congregation, my guilt was in overdrive. Guilt and happiness don't mix well.

Eventually, I came to realize that much of the guilt stemmed neither from God nor from the pastor. It was all me. I was trying to live up to some self-imposed definition of what a "good" church member looks like. Realizing that I probably wouldn't be the victim of God's vengeance if I didn't teach Sunday school, I began to set limits, with the church and with myself. I kept what was important: the praying, the devotionals, the sermons, and the fellowship. I continued to serve on one interesting committee and I finished the website. But I let go of those things that did not make me happy: taking on responsibilities I didn't want and being afraid of not living up to others' expectations. Once I let go of the guilt and was doing less, I was able to enjoy the sermons, the hymns, and the old ladies' stories again. I was able to return to the happiness I'd initially found. I think God's okay with me doing less for the church. No locusts or floods yet…

The Gift of Grace

My experiment with spirituality was coming along well. I'd conquered the Bible (kind of), I'd explored the writings of some other religious traditions, and I'd joined a church and surrounded myself with a community of believers. At this point in the experiment, I'd say that spirituality added to my happiness (with some small caveats). Wait, let me rephrase that. I think *religion* added to my happiness. The notion of spirituality is somewhat different. Spirituality is about more than church services, sermons, and books. It's something much bigger. Some may describe spirituality as a connection to the universe, finding solace in a higher power, or the feeling of belonging to something beyond oneself. For me, spirituality is about my relationship with God. And God's relationship with me. And I may be getting my terminology all wrong, but for this experiment, I'm simply going to refer to this relationship as God's grace. I consider grace to be the feeling that I'm loved and that I'm not alone. Grace is the belief that my life has meaning and purpose, chosen for me by God. Grace is about being able to let go of worry. Grace is knowing that things will work out eventually because there's a bigger picture. Grace is trusting that God can take care of the things that I can't. Same thing as spirituality? I don't know. Use whatever term you like, but for me, God's grace is the best way of describing things I don't understand.

I can't speak about grace from an academic sense, I can only talk about my personal experiences with a higher power. Some might argue that what I'm calling grace are merely coincidences, but I believe these are signs and messages from God continually reminding me that I'm loved and protected and that He does have a plan for me. At times, grace is presented to me in the form of something simple, like when the daily devotional pertains almost exactly to my situation. Or when the Sunday sermon answers a question I had earlier in the week. Or when the phone rings at the exact moment I'm feeling lonely. But, at other times, it's much bigger than that. Grace is directing me toward a path that changes my life, one I never would have chosen on my own. Some may say that it's just being in the right place at the right time. I believe God intervenes in our lives when we need His help the most, regardless of how stubborn, controlling, or fearful we've been. For me, this is grace.

Grace is incredibly difficult to explain, so let me offer a few examples of how God found me and shared His grace with me:

- ☺ I was having a hard time at work. A really hard time. I felt like I was screwing everything up. I also realized that I had no one at work to complain to about how much I was screwing up. The next morning, I cried all the way to work. Between the tears, I prayed. I asked for a friend. I asked to not feel so lonely and to have someone at work to provide me with some guidance. I just threw it all into the pot and said, "Please help me." When I arrived at work that morning, there was an e-mail from a co-worker asking if I would like to start a walking club with her. We agreed to take a walk at lunch and plan it out. While walking and talking, we were able to commiserate about how strange the office was. She gave me some advice, but it was also nice just to have a friend who understood. While I don't know that God normally works this quickly, He answered my prayer right away. Grace? Coincidence? Manifesting my desires? Who knows, but I went home that night feeling like God has my back. Completely.

☺ My daughter got an ear infection and couldn't go to school one morning. I still needed to teach at the university that day, so I couldn't stay home with her. I asked my mom to watch her for me, and when I arrived at my parents' house, my mom was in the process of having a heart attack and my dad wasn't home. I wouldn't have normally been there, but because of my daughter's ear infection and the fact that I couldn't cancel class, I ended up at their house that morning. Coincidence? Good timing? I don't really know, but I'm glad I was there.

☺ On a morning walk, I was stressing out about something I had to do later that day. When I saw a small white butterfly, I joked to myself that it was an angel sent from God to help me get through my rough day. As I turned the corner, suddenly there were small white butterflies everywhere. I was surrounded by them. Or was I surrounded by angels? Regardless, the rest of my day went beautifully. I had nothing to worry about.

☺ God seems to use my church members as reminders of His presence. Keep in mind that I live in a major metropolitan city. In a small town, stuff like this happens all the time, but to run into people you know in a big city like this is a lot less common...or is it? Regardless of the reason, here are some examples of God using my congregation to speak to me:

- When I got into a minor fender bender and had to file a police report, I was very upset and scared. When I walked in the police station, the volunteer taking reports that afternoon was a member of my church.

- When my daughter started preschool, I was quite anxious. The following Sunday, one of her teachers was sitting in a pew two rows behind me.
- One day I was freaking out about a dentist appointment, and when I walked in, a member of my church was sitting in the lobby. He told me jokes and eased my fears while I was waiting to see the dentist.
- Although I don't remember why, I was having a really bad morning. I stopped to get a bagel and ran into two members of my church who were having lunch at the bagel shop. They invited me to join them and filled me in on all the church gossip. It changed my mood immediately.

I have so many more stories like these, examples of times when something small, subtle, and unexpected changed the course of my day. I know these don't really qualify as "miracles" and could have been just coincidences, but they always seem to come at the perfect time.

While these are small examples, as I look back over my life, I can see how God put me exactly where I needed to be for the big things, too. I can see how God used other people to get me on the right track. I can also think of times when I was probably the answer to someone else's prayer. Things like this remind me that there's a plan in place. God knows what He's doing even when we don't. I'm sure that many of the things that have happened in my life weren't merely flukes but responses to my prayers. They let me know that God is listening. They help me to build my trust in Him and know that I really don't have anything to worry about. The universe really does have my back. When I can believe this, I am happy.

It's just hard to do. My human instincts often tell me to keep myself safe rather than trust in some unknown and unseen force. I'm a scientist and want to rely on logic and rationality, but I've also seen how the inexplicable keeps happening in my life. I really am more content when I rely on God's grace, but the world is too difficult sometimes. So what am I to do?

My daughter is the greatest theological teacher I've ever had. One night while saying prayers, she said to me, "Wait, I'm not done. I want to tell God something." She asked God to keep her balloons safe and not let any of them pop. Then she turned to me and said, "Let's see if God hears me." My heart broke at that moment. My rational mind knew full well that the balloons would probably pop. Popping is balloons' nature. It's just what they do. I tried to tell her that sometimes things happen even if we ask God for them not to. But she didn't want to hear it. The next day, she continued to play with the balloons happily, truly believing that both she and the balloons were safe.

Surprisingly, the balloons didn't pop. They just ran out of air. We watched them get smaller and smaller, but they never popped. She believed and God heard her. While probably not something anyone would call a miracle, it did remind me about trust. God loves us enough to pay attention to the things that are important to us. My daughter just had to remind me that sometimes God defies logic and rationality to take care of us. And when we can believe that, we can go about our day and our lives happily, knowing that we are safe.

This is where I struggle. I don't always have my daughter's conviction. As much as I want to believe that God will always take care of us, I still get very scared when things feel out of control. I tend to lose faith when bad stuff happens. I sometimes forget that when crap happens in my life, it isn't because God doesn't hear me. He always hears me. But that doesn't mean I'll get the answer I want (or think I want). Sometimes His answer is "no." Or His answer is "not yet." And sometimes when we get the "no," it's because there's a much more beautiful "yes" waiting. I can know this only by believing in God's grace. When I can accept this, I can find complete peace. I can go about happily playing with the balloons, unafraid of what might happen. It's just easier said than done. It's hard to relinquish control to God and believe that it's all going to work out. Even though I have seen God's miracles firsthand, I guess I still have some work to do. Maybe someday I, too, will believe those balloons won't pop and go happily about my life. Someday.

Let It Go

Grace is more than coincidences and building trust. It's helping us to let go of things weighing us down. It's a chance to treat each day as new. God's grace allows us a clean slate any time we ask. One morning, I was going through a traditional prayer routine, which included asking for forgiveness. But as I was praying, I suddenly became angry. *Why do I need to confess my sins and ask for forgiveness?* I thought. *I'm doing the best I can and trying to be good. So why do I need to feel guilty for not being good enough?* Years of being a therapist have taught me that unnecessary guilt is a pretty common affliction, especially among people who have done nothing wrong. I began to wonder about the point of asking for forgiveness. Is it just a tool of organized religion to get us to conform? Is this just another reason to fear God? A whole other series of thoughts and angry feelings arose. I really didn't need to add anger and guilt to my current playlist of worry, fear, and depression. I already had plenty of other negative emotions to dance to.

That afternoon, my reading for the day was Psalm 51 (coincidence?) If you're not familiar with this Psalm, it finds David praying to God after he's done something pretty bad, even by Bible standards (adultery, murder, coveting another's wife, you know, all the things God was pretty clear about not doing). When he realizes he's screwed up, he feels a lot of guilt and calls out to God. "Create in me a pure heart, O God, and renew a steadfast spirit within me … Restore to me the joy of your salvation and grant me a willing spirit, to sustain me." He was asking for a chance to try again, to keep going, to keep doing the things God had planned for him.

Suddenly, forgiveness made a lot more sense to me. It's not about guilt or shame but the opposite. Asking for forgiveness is actually about asking God to let you try again. "Give me a second chance, God. I won't let you down this time." Actually, we probably will, but at least we get the chance to try again. God doesn't want us to carry burdens of regret. A lot of our unhappiness comes from holding on to those things that no longer serve us. Forgiveness is about letting all of that go. What I had viewed as a punishing and oppressive practice is actually a gift.

Forgiveness is not for God; He has already forgiven us. The process of asking for forgiveness is for us, so that we can try again and keep going without dragging along all our old resentments. Being able to let go of those things that cause unhappiness is a pretty important part of being happy. Forgiveness allows us to do just that.

I often wonder if God made me a parent so that I could understand how much He loves us. I'm guessing He loves us infinitely more than I love my own child, but I do see the parallels. I think about how easily I forgive her. I think about how much easier our lives are when we forgive the mistakes and when we move forward without holding on to the hurt. I believe God wants the same for me. But I often get in the way of God's attempts to care for me. Sometimes when my daughter and I have had a rough day, she'll say to me, "I won't fight you anymore, I promise." Her words remind me that I often act as a defiant and rebellious child of God. I want to control things. I want to have things my own way on my own time line. I fight God and all that He is trying to do for me. But then I remember how much easier it is for both of us when I let go of those hurt feelings and just love my child. I now close out my evening prayer with the same phrase, asking forgiveness and saying, "I won't fight you tomorrow, I promise, God." I think we all know that neither my daughter's statement nor my statement is completely true, but our intentions are good. Luckily, I forgive her and God forgives me and we both get to keep trying. This is God's grace at work through the gift of forgiveness – the gift of letting go.

Findings and Analysis

While I didn't actually find any answers, there were many positives to this experiment. I was reminded of a loving God. I was able to better understand what Christians believe and why. I found a community of love and support. I was consistently reminded of God's grace. When I could relinquish enough control to accept this grace, I found happiness. Complete and total happiness.

But, I also came to see how religion can be a source of unhappiness. There were times when the church obligations and expectations caused stress, the Bible caused fear, and trying to appease an angry God caused worry. These things took away from my happiness. Once I was able to let go of the obligations of the church and the fear of upsetting God, things became easier. I had to stop trying so hard. I had to do less. I had to make space for God's grace to get in. It didn't even require any cleansing rituals or burnt offerings. I just had to say no to the things that were draining me of my time and energy, and let go of the things that were weighing me down. In its place, I had to accept grace and forgiveness. Seems like a good trade to me.

The problem is, while I know God's grace is there, I don't always rely on it. I still carry around my guilt and resentments. I still try to control things that I know I can do nothing about. I still fear life's difficulties and don't know if I'll have the strength to get through. I still worry how it's all going to work out. I know grace is an amazing gift from God, I'm just not completely sure how to accept it. If I could, I wouldn't need to do a happiness project.

To sum up my findings about spirituality and happiness, all I can say is, it's complicated. I set out to understand the nature of the universe and I didn't really find any answers. I don't know if angels exist. I don't know if the universe has our backs. I don't know why bad things happen to good people. I don't know if life is planned out or a series of random occurrences. Wrestling with some of these ideas helped me to understand my own happiness as it relates to my spiritual life, but it also brought up a lot more questions. I probably won't ever have any answers. For now, I'll just do my best to believe that the universe supports me and that there's a loving God who will take care of me. But I still don't read my horoscope—just in case.

Chapter 6

Do Nothing

Area of Inquiry: Meditation

Methods:

- Learn new and different meditation techniques
- Find a community of meditators and do group sits
- Practice meditation regularly
- Read books about meditation and mindfulness practices
- Enhance my ability to use my meditation skills "off the mat"

Happiness Quotient: 8/10

Experiment Design:

As I looked through the research around happiness, one thing came up over and over again: meditation. There are a number of benefits of meditation, especially as it relates to happiness and well-being. All the research says so. All the people who meditate say so. In fact, some would argue that meditation isn't just one of the factors that lead to a happy life but that it's the *direct path* to happiness. It's often said that meditation is the route to enlightenment and perfect peace. While reaching enlightenment seemed like too lofty an objective, I couldn't really say that I had explored happiness without at least trying meditation.

Beyond Therapy

Meditation isn't completely new to me. I'd been trained in mindfulness-based therapeutic treatments, but I don't think I "got it" at the time. When I would teach these therapeutic methods, I'd gloss over the mindfulness to get to the more active techniques. Although I saw great progress in my clients with some of these methods, I never really understood the reason for spending so much time focusing on the mindfulness portion. To me, that wasn't the interesting part. In fact, I always found it boring.

However, I wanted to let go of my judgments about meditation in the name of finding happiness. I figured that even if the meditation didn't work for me, I'd have the background to better understand the rationale for including mindfulness in mental health treatments. While I might not find nirvana, maybe I could at least be a better therapist.

Based on recommendations from other meditators and mental health practitioners, I started with Jon Kabat-Zinn's *Full Catastrophe Living*. I committed myself to practice and set aside time each day to do the exercises in the book. It took several attempts before I was able to get through even the most basic activities, but I'd made a commitment to meditating and was determined that I wouldn't give up.

After a few weeks, I gave up. I clearly sucked at meditation.

For some reason, though, it kept calling me back. And since everyone says it's the key to happiness, I kept trying. Every day I sat. And tried. But I still couldn't do it. Why was sitting on a cushion thinking about breathing so damn hard?

After finding it impossible to "just sit," I decided to skip ahead in the book to see if I could find something more interesting. No more sitting—I needed something to do. Then I found the body-scan meditation, which was a little more active. Although I was just lying there, focusing on my body gave my mind something to do. I was able to concentrate on different parts of my body and use my thoughts to describe what I felt. I learned how to recognize sensations without getting stuck on them, judging them, or trying to explain them. It was a good start.

Even after conquering a body scan or two, I still felt like I wasn't really meditating. My mind was still pretty wild, and despite my best efforts, I couldn't just sit. I went to YouTube to see what else I could find. I tried guided meditations, but to no avail. They weren't for me. The sessions seemed to take forever. My thoughts ran along the lines of "When are you going to say the next thing, talking person? Come on, let's move this along!" I also tried the walking meditation, with the same results. It was just too slow. I even tried a loving-kindness meditation. Sending peace and goodwill to others and myself sounded pretty easy. Wrong. In fact, I found myself getting angry during these meditations. I don't know for certain, but I'm guessing that anger isn't the intended outcome of a loving-kindness meditation. I began to think I just didn't have the patience for meditation. Or maybe I wasn't doing it right. I wasn't sure why I was having such a hard time.

Researchers go to the literature when they're stuck, so I headed to the local library. I found some books on meditation and read up. I learned that most meditators experience the same thing I was struggling with. Apparently, most people aren't that great at meditation (at least not at first). This gave me some validation. Turns out that all minds, not just mine, are unruly beasts.

Knowing I wasn't alone, I made a new commitment to practice meditation, but this time I gave myself permission to suck at it. Every day, I sat. And, of course, I thought. I had so many thoughts. I gently acknowledged those thoughts and began counting my breaths. And then I'd think again. And then I'd breathe and count again. I did this over and over and over. The best I could do was to sit while my mind did what it does and to then try redirecting it. Oddly, this daily tug-of-war with my brain soon became my favorite part of the day.

Although I still wasn't great at it, I'd begun to appreciate meditation. It helped me to see that thoughts are just thoughts. That's it. Why couldn't someone have told me this, like, twenty years ago? How much anxiety it would have saved me! Meditation helped me redefine my relationship with the thoughts. The more I practiced, the more comfortable I became with letting them come and go. They weren't there to scare me, they were just there. I learned to sit as song lyrics, irrational fears, important revelations, pointless problems, TV show plots, and plans for what I was going to eat later in the day played in my head. I also learned to sit through some painful things (both physically and mentally) without doing a single thing. One of the biggest benefits of my practice is that it made me feel less helpless. Meditation is the action of inaction. It gave me a place to put my energy while I let things settle. It allowed me to reset myself. It gave me permission to just be without solving every single problem that popped into my head. When everything felt out of control around me, I could gain some control by watching my breath and noticing my thoughts. It gave me something to do when there was absolutely nothing I could do. I'm finding that meditation is full of contradictions like that.

Eventually, I was getting benefit not just during my meditation times but at other times as well. Somehow, the world began to seem different to me. When my mind wasn't cluttered with useless thoughts, I was able to see things I'd never seen before. I've lived in my neighborhood for over fifteen years, but every day I saw something I'd never noticed. I found myself being more patient (or at least doing a better job of noticing when I was being impatient). For the first time in a long time, things had slowed down. It felt nice.

Despite getting some benefits from meditation, I still struggled with my thought process both on and off the mat. I would forget about meditation at the times I needed it the most. I could still become consumed by fear and worry. Some days, I couldn't even meditate at all. It seemed like a lot of work for a few moments of peace. Although it was nice to feel somewhat calmer, I surely wasn't happier. I didn't completely understand how meditation led to happiness. Was I missing something? I couldn't shake the feeling that maybe there was more to the story.

The Rest of the Story

Evidently there is more to the story. A lot more. As I began looking into meditation, I learned that there are probably thousands of ways to meditate beyond just sitting and breathing. There are lots of ways to incorporate these practices into day-to-day living. There are people around the world who spend all day in meditation and mindfulness practices, and have found happiness in doing so. Maybe I just needed to try some different techniques. Wanting to be a better meditator creates attachment and kind of defeats the purpose of meditation, so I instead decided to make it my objective to expand my meditation repertoire. The big question was how. I'd already read several books and spent some time on YouTube, and yet, for some reason, that didn't help me grow.

When researchers aren't finding the answers they need in the literature, they seek out a content expert. Maybe that's what I needed: an expert meditator, a guru, a teacher. I needed the personal touch. I began looking for people or places that could help me with meditation. Specifically:

- I looked up meditation organizations online.
- I drove by a place that offered daily sitting meditations.
- I talked to my parents about one of their neighbors who meditates regularly.
- I commented on a Facebook picture of my uncle's new meditation room.
- I liked the YouTube channel of a local meditation teacher.
- I read a copy of a magazine called Mindful that I borrowed from a friend.
- I e-mailed the local Zen Center to inquire about its services.

All these things and I was not a better meditator yet. Hmmm....

The following week, I received an e-mail response from the Zen Center saying that it offered daily sittings but that for beginner sits, I should already be able to sit "relatively still" for thirty-five minutes, followed by fifteen minutes of walking meditation and then another thirty-five-minute sit. Yeah, probably not going to happen. I don't time myself, but I'm pretty sure that thirty-five minutes would be a reach for me.

A coworker suggested I contact the local Buddhist temple, but the last time I was in a Buddhist temple, I accidentally set myself on fire, so I wasn't sure that was a good idea.[3] Still, I was open to giving it a try, so I called. The temple had meditation offerings similar to the Zen Center's, meaning I'd need to be very still for long periods of time. It didn't really offer training or teaching but rather an opportunity to sit with others.

Both the Zen Center and the Buddhist Temple informed me that I also had the option to attend a ten-day silent retreat. If I couldn't sit for thirty-five minutes, how on earth would I be able to sit for ten days? Clearly, I needed to find something more remedial.

I reached out to a friend who teaches yoga and does massage and bodywork and asked her if she knew of a teacher who might be able to help me learn meditation. Did she know of anyone who could offer a kindergarten-level class for meditators? "Yes, me!" she said and agreed to take me on as a student. I'd found my guru.

As would be expected, we spent some time sitting. But, I also learned some new things, too. My guru taught me guided meditations and different breathing techniques. We used movement, music, candles/light, and rocks. I learned mantras and chants and other such things that could help distract my mind. I began using them even when I wasn't meditating. I found myself driving through a rainstorm

---

3 Okay, here's the story. We went there for a religious studies class. We were given a tour and joined in a short sitting meditation to see what it was like. The monks gave us incense to hold, which was part of the process. During the meditation, one of the embers from the incense fell onto my sleeve. As I was trying to be quiet and respectful, my sweatshirt began smoking. I tried to politely put it out, but it's a little awkward to douse a fire and just sit at the same time. What's the protocol for catching on fire during meditation? I didn't know. I still don't. So much left to learn.

chanting, "Ek Ong Kar," which helped prevent me from getting too distressed or imagining all the horrible things that could happen. At night, "Om mani padme hum" helped me to drift off to sleep.

We also explored meditation techniques for enhancing my religious practices. She taught me about techniques of Lectio Divina, Taizé, and contemplative prayer, which use scripture as the basis for the meditation practice. I enjoyed these techniques so much that I've been pestering my pastor for the past year to add them to the church's worship schedule.

The more I learned, the more I loved it. I now understood how people could meditate for hours or days at a time. In fact, I was strongly considering running off and joining a Buddhist monastery. Maybe a long-term goal, but in the meantime, I turned my focus to trying to implement meditation or mindfulness practices throughout the day. I tried to be mindful and present when eating, walking, or talking to others. When I got flustered at work, I would close my door and meditate. Traffic stressing me out? That became the perfect time for a contemplative prayer. When my daughter was driving me crazy, I would have her dance or chant with me. I accepted emotions as they came and went. I learned how to use these different techniques to get "off the mat" benefits that I could use throughout my day. I finally felt like I could just let my thoughts go. For the first time, I felt like my mind and I no longer had to be enemies. And that made me really happy.

Findings and Analysis

In Dan Harris's book *10% Happier*, he comes to the realization that meditation is nice but it doesn't solve all the world's problems. That's true. Meditation doesn't directly solve any problems. But it does make space for problems to be solved (if they even need to be solved.) Most of the problems that I took to my meditation cushion had no solutions, in part because they weren't really even problems to begin with.

I see why meditation is included in all the happiness literature. It does bring peace, even if it's in small moments. It's helped me to look at the world differently. It's helped to make me more patient, which has helped my relationships. It provides a brief respite from the noise in my head. When I can't do anything else to deal with my problems, my pain, or my stress, I can meditate. Those times when I can incorporate meditation techniques into my day, even in tiny spaces, the world didn't seem so overwhelming. Doing nothing made me happier than I thought it would.

However, meditation is also really hard to do, which is why I didn't rate it higher on the happiness quotient. It's hard to remember to use the techniques when I need them the most. It's hard to just sit and breathe. There are some days I can't meditate at all, regardless of how hard I try. It's hard to make space to be quiet in a world that demands that we be busy. Doing nothing is surprisingly hard.

Although this experiment took a lot more work than I expected, I'm glad I stuck with it. I love the simplicity and complexity of meditation. I love how all these contradictory ideas can exist all together at the same time, which has taught me to be more comfortable with other contradictions in my life and in the world. I plan to keep doing nothing. Every morning, I start with a body scan and a loving-kindness meditation. I close my days with a Lectio Divina and the Ignatian Spiritual Exercises. And sometimes during the day I'll just sit. For no reason at all. I can honestly say that those times are my favorite parts of the day. Just maybe I'll work my way up to the ten-day silent retreats. Ten full days of silence should provide me just enough time to solve all the problems of the world—or, remember every single one-hit wonder of the '80s. Let's see where this goes.

Chapter 7

The Balancing Act

Area of Inquiry: Figure out work/life balance

Methods:

- Develop a work-at-home schedule
- Make some decisions about taking on additional work
- Spend more quality time with my daughter
- Create time for personal activities
- Explore part-time options
- Determine what I want to be when I grow up

Happiness Quotient: 7/10

Experiment Design:

When I chose this subject, it was primarily a way to assuage my guilt because my daughter was in day care. In my mind, finding the balance between working and taking care of my child was the definition of work/life balance. However, as I struggled with this topic, I realized that I was missing the bigger picture. In addition to the ethical conundrum of how I was going to both work and raise my child, I wanted to be able to do other things, too. What about fun? What about spending time with friends? What about family commitments? What about time to myself to read, exercise, and sleep? I wanted to take some time to determine if I could find happiness while having it all. Could I bring home the bacon and fry it up in a pan? I was going to do my best to find out.

The research literature is varied on the role of work in relation to happiness. One book I read indicated that work is the most important factor in happiness, even going so far as to suggest that the secret to happiness among older adults is to never retire. While this might be a bit of an extreme suggestion, there is some support in the literature for finding happiness through working. One study indicated that people who are happy in their jobs also tend to be happy in other areas of their lives. Those who enjoy their jobs suffer from less burnout and less stress and enjoy a greater sense of personal accomplishment and achievement.

While work can provide happiness, it is also the source of a lot of unhappiness. A recent study indicated that Americans reported their jobs as their primary source of stress. Workload concerns, conflicts with bosses and co-workers, long commutes, and spending time away from family were cited most often as the specific reasons. It makes sense that workers are stressed. Americans are working longer hours, taking fewer vacations, and are perpetually connected to their jobs. And, despite the suggestion that we might be happier if we never retire, some of the research actually says differently. In longitudinal happiness studies, older adults routinely cite the time right after retiring as their happiest.

At the time of this experiment, I was working for a social service research company. My job was essentially to analyze data and write reports. If you think that sounds pretty boring, you would be correct. When one of my co-workers from a different department asked if she could shadow me one day, I told her my job is mostly sitting in my office cussing or crying. I was only partially kidding. Yeah, it was boring, but it was also really flexible. Plus, it provided a routine for the week, gave me something to do, and supplied a little bit of cash to pay the contractor and the housekeeper. It was also my first full-time job since having my daughter, so it was also a big change. I hadn't worked more than a few hours a week since becoming a mom, and I soon learned that work and career are completely different when one is a parent. I'd gone from being fully committed to my workplace to being fully committed to my daughter to now trying to figure out how I could be fully committed to both. I wasn't sure how I was going to give them each 100%. Since I'm a statistician, I know how probabilities and percentages work, and even with the fanciest mathematical techniques, the chances of my being able to give both places my all was pretty low. Something was going to have to give. But what? That's what I tried to figure out with this experiment.

Work/Life Balance

Before I had a child, I never thought of such things as work/life balance. There was no balance. There was just work. I was okay with this. I like working. Work has always been a big part of my happiness. It provided me with emotional and mental stimulation. I enjoyed my co-workers and always found a way to have fun. My jobs were important and meaningful. Looking back, maybe I should have taken more time to travel or spend time with my family. Maybe I should have taken samba dance lessons or gone camping. At the time, I didn't think of these things because I never felt like I was missing anything. I never felt any kind of imbalance at all.

When my daughter was born, I decided to stay home with her. I didn't feel as if I had any other choice. She needed me. I gave corporate America the middle finger and said, "You'll have to figure out how to keep America running without me!" When I made that decision, I didn't yet know that being a stay-at-home mom is by far the hardest job ever. It was the most work I've ever done in my life. And it was often boring and usually pretty lonely. But, we had complete freedom to do whatever we wanted. It was awesome and awful at the same time.

Right before my daughter turned three, something magical happened. We decided she might benefit from some socialization and structure, so, on Monday and Wednesday mornings, I dropped her off at preschool to play with friends, learn how to line up, and do something other than binge-watch *Handy Manny* with me all day. While she was at school, I could do whatever I wanted. For the first time since she'd been born, I had my own time. It was only four hours a week, but it was the most wonderful four hours ever. Sometimes I would run errands or take care of business. Other times, I would volunteer or go for a walk or just sit in a coffee shop and stare out the window. This was the kind of balance I needed.

As she became more comfortable in preschool, I decided that maybe it was time for me to go back to work. I thought I could probably benefit from some socialization and structure, too. I loved her school and felt like it would be okay for her to be there for more than a few hours a week, so I started looking for part-time work.

It's complicated how I went from four hours of freedom to working full time, but long story short, I became a working mom. For anyone who cares to argue and debate, being a stay-at-home mom was way harder. But that's not to say this working mom thing isn't pretty challenging, too. In the past, I'd worked as hard and as long as I wanted, but not anymore. The school closes at six. And sometimes my daughter gets sick. And she has Halloween parties and Valentine's parties and family breakfast day. Every single morning, I had to get her belly full and her bladder empty, get her dressed, find the purple stuffed unicorn for nap time, get through the separation-anxiety good-byes and then try to make my eight-thirty meeting on the other side of town. By the end of the day, I was far more worried about picking her up on time than anything I was working on. I began ignoring e-mails and walking out of meetings early to avoid evening traffic. I was probably not going to win employee of the year any time soon. Despite my best efforts, I was still sometimes late, arriving to a child in tears. Mother of the year wasn't looking good either.

In addition to working through the basic logistics, I found another side effect of being a working parent: It was hard to be away from her for forty hours a week. I missed her—a lot. I didn't like missing out on some of the big moments of her life. I even began missing *Handy Manny*, too.

The Balancing Act

As the year progressed, I could recognize that I wasn't really happy with the situation. I could tell she wasn't happy either. Our morning good-byes became more difficult and she frequently spent the evening in tears. She would ask me to pick her up early the next day. Although I was doing okay at work and she loved her school, I wondered if it was all too much.

I tried other things to give her a little bit of a break from school, like having her go to my parents' house one day a week. She went in her pajamas and spent the day eating cookies and playing games with her grandparents. My husband would also occasionally flex his schedule to pick her up early so they could hang out. I even used up some of my vacation days to give us a chance to visit the zoo and the museum just like we used to do.

Although my main concern was my daughter, I also wanted some time to do some of the other things I'd previously fit into my glorious four hours of freedom. I wanted to volunteer at her school. I wanted to help out at the church. I wanted to participate in a moms group. I wanted to teach a class or two at the School of Social Work at the local university. When I tried to add these in, though, the work/life balance thing became a lot more complicated. I was sure I could make it work. I just needed more hours in the day. I was used to manipulating numbers, and I just needed to think through how to fit everything I wanted to do into my allotted time.

Luckily, my job offered several "family-friendly" policies. Maybe if I took advantage of some of them, I could care for my daughter, do some of the other things I wanted to do, and get my work done. Lots of people with more kids and less flexible jobs pulled it off. It was just a matter of figuring out the formula. I had 168 hours each week to work with. Surely that's enough time for work and play. I'd soon be juggling everything better than a circus performer. Go ahead, throw in the chain saws and the flaming batons—I got this.

I just needed a better plan. Here were my ideas for how I was going to get this work/life thing into balance:

Plan #1 – Work from Home

My first attempt was to use a work-at-home day. I figured my daughter could just hang out with me while I worked. It was the perfect answer. We could be together but I could still get my projects done. Genius.

Any of you who have tried to get anything done with a preschooler around are now laughing quite heartily at my naiveté. I don't know why I thought I would be able to do anything with her at home with me. For example, during one of my conference calls, she yelled, "Mom, come look how big my poop is! It's giant!" She helped to "decorate" one of my reports with stickers. She would get on to my work computer to play ABC mouse… but it wasn't ABC mouse. It was my work discussion board. While these things were frustrating, the bigger problem was that most days, she would continually ask me when I would be done working. I didn't get to spend more time with her as I planned, rather, I usually ended up just turning on a video while I tried to get my work done. I'm not sure that was any better than sending her to day care.

I liked my work-at-home day and kept it, but I ended up taking her back to day care so I could actually get some work done. I saved about forty-five minutes a day by not commuting to and from the office, but I didn't really gain much time with my daughter or time for myself. I typically ended up just using that extra forty-five minutes to scroll Facebook. All this just made me feel guiltier.

Plan #2 – Flex Time

Instead of keeping her home with me during the day, I figured I'd maximize our time together by flexing my work time. My plan was to get up early and work while she was still in bed. Then I'd pick her up early from school and we'd spend the afternoon doing fun things. While it was a great idea, in practice it didn't quite work. Rather than working less, I felt like I was working all the time. Because my days were interrupted, I felt like my entire day was spent working. I'd work from five thirty to eight thirty in the morning, get her up, take her to school for a bit, play with her in the afternoon and then do more work after she went to bed. I'd take my computer into the bathroom and type while she was in the bath. I read my tablet while we were at the playground. With this disrupted schedule, I wasn't able to do everything that needed to be done, so I ended up also working on Saturday and Sunday mornings, hoping my daughter would sleep in really late. Suddenly I had no days off. And when there were emergencies or deadlines at work, I resorted to letting her watch hours upon hours of silly YouTube videos so I could finish things up. I didn't even have time to scroll Facebook anymore. This wasn't really working either.

Plan #3 – Part Time

When my child began kissing the tablet good night and trying to make her own YouTube videos, I knew that the days of using the Internet as a babysitter were over. I needed to come up with a different plan. I thought that maybe if I had an additional day off each week, this would give me some time to take her to the zoo or the museum or the park or really anything that didn't involve a television, so I requested to go part time. However, this didn't really help much. I was working almost as much as before, but getting paid less. I had an official "day off," but still responded to e-mails and even agreed to meetings on those days. I used the rest of my "day off" to teach and volunteer, but these commitments meant my daughter was still in day care during this time. Even with an extra day, things just weren't feeling very balanced. Rather, I felt like I was only precariously holding everything together.

I have no idea how families make this work. It's not like mine is a unique struggle. I'm in a much better position than most people: my job is pretty flexible, I have support from my husband and parents, and I have an easy, healthy kid. But no matter how hard I tried, I just couldn't find the balance. Maybe returning to being a stay-at-home mom was my best option. Maybe I'd had it right all along.

But, I couldn't just quit. Not yet.

As soon as I said I needed to make some decisions about work, the company my husband worked for declared bankruptcy. Until we knew if he was going to have a job, I had to stay put. We couldn't really risk being without a consistent paycheck and health insurance. At that moment, I realized how other families make it work—they don't have any other choice.

Making It Work (Kinda)

My husband spent the summer looking for other jobs while I kept working. He interviewed for quite a few positions, some of which he turned down partly because of our daughter. He wanted her to have access to good schools and her grandparents. If we didn't have her, we could go pretty much anywhere in the country and do whatever we wanted, but there's so much more to consider when children are involved. I offered him the option to be a stay-at-home dad while I took on a higher-paying job, but he's someone who needs to work. His happiness is tied to being productive. So he kept looking.

Eventually, he found a new job. But while it provides a paycheck and health insurance, it also includes an hour-long commute each way. And he has to work weekends. And holidays. He can't help with our daughter as much as he had before, which adds to my parenting responsibilities. While I was relieved that he'd found employment, it turned out to be just another way to knock things out of balance.

As if I wasn't already struggling with my balance, the universe decided to toss me a couple of flaming batons. My mom had some health issues and ended up in the hospital. In addition to trying to figure out how to get my work done and pay some attention to my child, I also now needed to help my parents. It was all too much.

The strange thing was, I was doing all of this for a job I didn't even enjoy. And it turns out I wasn't that good at it either. I was getting feedback that my work wasn't done in the way my employer wanted. And I burned my bagel in the toaster, which made the kitchen smell. And I kept borrowing people's pens and not returning them. And I never refilled the candy bowl on my desk with the good kinds of candy. And my division took last place in the relay race at the company retreat because I dropped the egg off the spoon. I was far from the model employee. But unlike in previous employment, I wasn't interested in doing my job better. I didn't care about my mistakes. I didn't really care about the job at all. I began to question why I was putting so much energy into trying to make it fit into my life. Why was I allowing it to take away from those things that do make me happy? If something has to give, shouldn't I keep the things that I actually care about?

Vocation and Profession

I remember watching an episode of *Boston Legal* or some other law show where the firm won its case, as is expected on these types of shows. But in an unusual twist, at the end of the show the firm's lawyer sat and talked with the opposing lawyer, who revealed that he had never won a case. Not one single case in his thirty-year legal career. He went on to share that he didn't even like being a lawyer, but didn't know what else he would do. I began to wonder why he would stay in a profession he didn't like and wasn't good at. When the other lawyer asked him that exact question, he said because it was what he had trained to do. Everyone expected him to be a lawyer. It was what he'd always done, and he didn't know anything else. He just assumed he had to keep doing it. He didn't realize he had options. I decided then and there that I never wanted to be that guy. I promised myself back then that I would not spend my life in a job I don't like and that I am not good at. Yet here I was.

After some introspection, I came to realize that while my job was okay, it wasn't my vocation. I'm a person who needs my profession to provide me with more than a paycheck. I want to feel like I'm making a difference. I want to have fun. I want to love and be loved. I want to do good in the world. Despite the flexibility and the family-friendly policies, there was a lot missing from my job. I had a hard time connecting with my co-workers. I couldn't see how my work was changing the world. And no one laughed at my statistics jokes, not even the really funny ones. If I was going to give my time and energy to something, shouldn't I choose those things I actually care about?

This work/life balance experiment was a bust. I couldn't find the balance, in part because I didn't want to. This particular job wasn't worth it to me. But since I'm not near retirement and my daughter is not ready to leave for college, I was still going to have to figure this out. Could I find a job that I enjoyed and cared about while still having the time and energy for other things in my life? Could I ever find the balance?

What Do You Want to Be When You Grow Up?

I wasn't sure what to do. What would make me happy? My devotional for that week was about a man who was considering leaving his job to start a personal project. As he was trying to make the decision, he made a list of all the things that made him happy. Then he made a list of all the thing he did in his current job. They didn't match. Then he made a list of all the things he'd be doing if he took a risk and started a missionary training program. This list matched the list of things that made him happy.

It was a good idea, so I did the same thing. I made a list of all the things that made me happy in my professional life. This was my list:

- Teaching and learning
- Talking to people and helping them find hope
- Being silly or creative
- Having fun with co-workers
- Writing and creating

I wasn't doing any of these things in my existing job, so I started a job search. I applied for some faculty positions where I could teach.

I applied for some clinical jobs where I could spend some time with people. I even applied for a few research positions that were more in line with my interest areas. I was offered some of the jobs, but none of them had the flexibility that I needed to work but also take care of my daughter, help my parents, finish the laundry, and allow me enough time to catch up on Netflix. What's a girl to do?

Although I couldn't find the perfect job, I went ahead and resigned from my research position. I decided that it simply wasn't worth it. I often think of that poor lawyer on the TV show and thank him for teaching me such a valuable lesson.

After I stopped working, I resumed my role as stay-at-home mom. This made my daughter happier, which made me happier. She still went to preschool a few mornings a week and was delighted when I picked her up before nap. We were able to help out my parents, and we even made it to the museum a few times. I was able to volunteer, spend time working at the church, and go skiing. I had to be a little more careful with money, which meant less eating out, no more housekeeper, and curbing our Build-A-Bear addiction, but it was worth every penny.

Interestingly, right after I stopped working, four parents from the preschool told me they'd decided to stay at home with their children as well. They told me they'd tried working and couldn't do it all either. They shared with me their difficulties with balance and said that any extra income they were forgoing wasn't worth the stress. I knew exactly what they meant. While I felt a little bad that other families had to make this tough decision, I also took solace in knowing that I wasn't alone. Maybe this problem is bigger than just me.

What Comes Next

What comes next? I didn't know. I had already left my job and couldn't find a new one that met my needs, so I did nothing. And when I did nothing, the answer came to me. While at a social event, as is typical upon meeting new people, others asked me what I did for a living. I automatically started to say, "I'm not working right now," but then I caught myself. Instead, I decided to talk about my happiness experiments and replied, "I study happiness." I got a few strange stares, but then I got lots of questions. People wanted to know what that meant. They wanted to know what I'd learned. They wanted to know why some people are happy and others aren't. They wanted to know what they could do to become happier. They were genuinely curious. Soon, this was happening everywhere I went. It seems happiness research is a well-received occupation choice. Could this be my job?

My Lectio Divina later that week led me to a verse to help me answer the question. Ecclesiastes 3 says, "I know that there is nothing better for people than to be happy and to do good while they live." Then there was something about being happy in one's work. Good enough for justification for me. Although it's not technically a "job," my new vocation is to talk to people about happiness. I read about happiness. I write about happiness. I run groups to help people understand happiness. I analyze data about happiness. I think about ways to help others to explore their own happiness. I find my happy by helping others know about happy. It's a great job to have. And I didn't even know it existed. Best of all, I don't have to give up any time with my daughter to do it.

Findings and Analysis

As a whole, this topic was very challenging but well worth the exploration. I realize that work can make some people happy and make others miserable. For some, it makes no difference at all. As for me, I'm happiest when I'm in a job where I feel like I'm doing some good while also having some fun. I know those jobs exist, but it also means I might have to give up time with my daughter and some of my freedom. I don't know that it's a fair trade.

I recognize that for many, the question isn't just about balance. I know I'm lucky in that I could just quit my job. I have good financial management skills, some savings, and a very patient and understanding husband, so I could take some time to figure things out. I also have job skills and a good education, so I have a lot of options when it comes to finding a job where I might be able to find meaning and balance. I'm fully aware of my privilege in having the freedom to explore my options without having my heat turned off or losing my health insurance. I know that not everyone can do this. But for those who feel stuck, I want to remind you that you may have more options than you think. Don't be that lawyer from the TV show.

As for me, I do find a lot of happiness from working and I want to be a productive and contributing member of society. However, I don't think I can expect to find all of my meaning in the workplace anymore. There are other important things in my life that also need my attention. In order to balance it all, I had to completely rethink work. I had to be creative and be willing to take some risks. I had to move away from traditional work roles and create something that fit my life and all that I wanted to do. Doing less, working less, and creating the space to figure out my vocation helped me to figure out where working fits into my life. While I was watching TV one afternoon (I had a little extra time to do that once I'd quit), Mike Rowe from the show *Dirty Jobs* said, "Happiness doesn't come from a job. It comes from knowing what you truly value and behaving in a manner consistent with those beliefs." I'm trying my best to do just that.

Exploring work as part of a happiness experiment helped me to understand how my values have shifted since becoming a parent. The experiment forced me to align myself with those goals. It ended up being less about "what do I want to be when I grow up" and more about evaluating what things are worthy of my time. I had to let go of notions that a job would make me happy. That's not to say I can't enjoy my employment, I'm just hoping I can find a way to prioritize my time so that my life is more balanced and that enjoyment comes from lots of places.

I'm sure my work life will change at some point, but for now, my happiness research work is going well. I get to spend my days thinking and writing about happiness. I also get to be with my child, volunteer at her school, do work at the church, help out my parents, take a walk by myself, and occasionally sneak away for an episode of *The Office*, just for a reminder of what I'm missing.

Chapter 8

It's All Fun and Games

Area of Inquiry: Have Fun

Methods:

- Play
- Get outside
- Make jokes
- Find a regular club/group/activity that's fun
- Enjoy downtime with leisure activities
- Take myself less seriously

Happiness Quotient: 10/10

Experiment Design:

Who can have happiness without a little fun and laughter? People who know me well can attest that I love to have fun. They might even describe me as a bit of a goofball. In new or professional situations, I can come off as quiet and serious, but the real me, the one I like the best, is a little crazy. I love to make jokes. I love to laugh. I love to do things that make me look foolish. I like to be playful and find the humor in life. This person, the fool, has been missing for a while. Everything that's happened over the past few years has made me serious. But being serious isn't really who I am. This experiment was an attempt to find my silly side again.

The research around fun and leisure-time activities was mixed. Part of the problem was that in the literature, the term *fun* wasn't well-defined. For some people, going bowling is fun. For others, riding roller-coasters is fun. There's a wide variation in the types of fun, all of which are personally defined, making the concept a little hard to measure. Maybe because of this, there was no real consistency in the literature around happiness and fun. Some of the studies showed that those who participated in many fun activities reported higher levels of happiness. In other cases, there was no relationship. One study even indicated that sometimes leisure activities were a source of unhappiness, as they created extra obligations, such as having to show up to an event so as not to let down other team members. As a whole, the research didn't really offer me much guidance about what to expect if I tried having fun. I was on my own with this one.

The Good Old Days

In the past, having fun wasn't something I necessarily needed to think about. It was just something I did. I went skiing regularly. I spent a lot of time on my bike and taking hikes. I played hockey. I participated in a weekly trivia contest. I got lost in corn mazes and went to haunted houses. I could find fun just about anywhere. After my daughter was born, some of these things took a backseat. I still tried to have fun, but kid fun. We went to the zoo and the museum. We played in the sand and painted pictures. We went to the playground almost every day. But when I got sick, I didn't have the energy for any of these things anymore, so we mostly hung out in the house, doing a lot of nothing. It wasn't fun. After I began to feel better, I wanted to do fun things again, but I never really did. Now that I had made the commitment to myself to be happy, I was going to make fun a priority.

When I chose to experiment with this, I was surprised that I couldn't just immediately turn on the fun. I had a few humorous Facebook posts, but beyond that, having fun didn't come quite as easily anymore. I didn't expect having fun to be quite so much work. I didn't know what fun things to do. I couldn't find the time. It took too much effort. These were my excuses. I needed to stop waiting for fun to just happen. I needed to go looking for it.

Family Fun

Having fun as a family seemed like an easy place to start. The good thing about having a preschooler in the house is that they're almost always up for fun. Plus, it gave me a good excuse to do things for "her sake."

We started small. For example, after I would pick her up from school, rather than just going home and watching TV, we would go to the park or go get ice cream. We'd turn on the radio and have dance parties before bed. We played with dolls, raced cars around the house, and built LEGO castles. It was a nice start. It felt easy. It was fun.

Then we ventured out of the neighborhood. I renewed all my museum passes and we hit the town. It was fun to see my daughter experience many of the old haunts with fresh eyes. She was also now old enough to do many of the activities at the Children's Museum, so that became our new favorite. We began hiking as a family, and my daughter even decided to give fishing a try.

This experiment was not really about providing activities for my daughter to have fun, I wanted to have fun, too. So I played with her. I went up and down slides and played on the swings. I finger-painted and splashed in the water. We went sledding and had snowball fights. I just let loose and enjoyed myself. I allowed myself be the carefree preschooler right along with her. The more I played, the more I noticed my awesome trying to creep back in. At one point while climbing on the playground, I noticed glimpses of the silly me and whispered to myself, "Oh, there you are." Who knew that all I needed was to enjoy myself a little?

That summer, my nephews, ages nine and eleven, stayed with us and we really had fun. These boys are adventurers and risk-takers. They wanted to try new things, so that's what we did. We climbed rocks and attempted to learn to paddleboard. We strapped on Rollerblades and hit the skate park. We played glow-in-the-dark mini-golf and went to rock-n-roll bowling. And they somehow talked me into going to the water park, where I even went down the fastest water slide. I think it was good for me to have them around because it forced me to have bigger fun.

They also helped us to establish a new family tradition, a fun activity to get us out of the house: Pokémon Go. If you're not familiar with the game, it's an app that uses location and allows you to hunt and capture virtual Pokémon. The real benefit of the game is that you have to move to make it work. You have to get out and walk. When my nephews suggested we play it, we gave it a try, and we all had fun walking around different parks, trying to locate Pokémon and build our collections. After my nephews went home, my daughter and I continued playing and taking a daily walk to go Pokémon hunting. Eventually, though, my daughter developed a horrible addiction to it, but that's another story for another day. I just feel lucky that we were able to break the habit before she ended up on the street, stealing people's phones to try to "just catch one more."

Playful Parenting

I found that the more time I spent having fun with my child, the easier parenting became. I began to use fun to my advantage. Need her to get moving? Have a race. Need to get her into the bath? Pretend to be mermaids. Can't get her to clean up her toys? Create a scavenger hunt for all the toys "hidden" in the house. Won't get dressed? Dress her stuffed animals in clothes and have a fashion show.

Having fun together cut down on the arguing and made both our lives easier. When she was upset, I found that making jokes or distracting her with something silly worked far better than trying to console her. I laughed when she fell down, so she'd laugh, too. I think it helped both of us to take ourselves less seriously. We also began to use play to help her solve problems. At one point, she was having a hard time going to school, so I suggested we play it out. We played school over and over again, changing roles and changing scenarios. We played it until she was ready to move on to something else. Getting her to school was no longer as big a deal when I could remind her how brave rainbow bunny was on his first day of school.

Bedtime with a preschooler is typically challenging, so I figured why not make bedtime fun, too? We started doing bedtime stories. Sometimes she'd tell them, sometimes I would, but they always ended with the characters in the story being so tired from their adventures that they just fell asleep. This was a lot more fun than arguing about what time it was and how tired she would be in the morning or trying to find consequences that would actually motivate her to stay in bed.

With play, I seemed to be able to get her to do what needed to be done. I'd become a playful-parenting badass. *I'm totally going to write a book about this*, I thought. Then one night while playing monsters to get my daughter into pajamas, she kicked me square in the face. "Can't let the monsters get you" was her justification. Maybe I have some details to work out before I write that book.

Fun at Work

Since I was spending half my waking hours at work, I figured I might as well try to enjoy it a little. There's not much that's funny about analyzing data, though. I tried really hard, but I just couldn't come up with any statistics jokes that other people thought were funny. Maybe it wasn't my jokes, though—maybe statisticians don't have a sense of humor. Maybe there's a good reason that statistics jokes are an untapped market.

At any rate, I still wanted to bring a little levity into an otherwise tedious day, so I engaged one of my co-workers who also liked fun. We started the Friday lunch club. She'd send out funny memes, to which I would respond with other funny memes. It was only a few laughs on Friday morning, but it typically helped my mood. We also went on walks during our lunch breaks, finding things to laugh about along the way. She was a fun person. It's easy to have fun when you're around fun people. But by the end of summer, she took another job and left the company. My playmate was gone. I had to think of something else to get me through the day. I broke up the day by hopping onto Facebook or Twitter to make jokes with other funny people. Sometimes I'd watch funny cat videos. I began listening to comedy podcasts or *Saturday Night Live* skits while doing my work. It wasn't quite the same as laughing with my friends, but a little bit of fun made the workday easier.

The Perils of Play

Although I was enjoying myself, having this much fun came with some costs: sunburns, sore muscles, mosquito bites, scraped knees, bee stings, and blisters. I cut my hand on sequins from playing dress-up, and I'm pretty sure I banged my head on every slide in the city. (When did playground equipment get so small?) I was sometimes in pain after my adventures, and my chiropractor informed me it was because terrain parks weren't intended for people with forty-year-old hips. Was having fun worth all the risk?

The answer to this question lies in my attitude. One part of this experiment was an attempt to take myself and the world less seriously. I used to be able to find the humor in almost any situation, and I really needed to get that ability back. One afternoon my daughter and I were at a park and she wanted to play in the small stream. When she took off her socks and shoes, one of the shoes fell into the stream and I tried to reach it but couldn't. It was floating away quickly, and I knew the only way to save it was to step into the stream myself. This would mean sloshing around in soaked shoes and wet pants, but what other choice did I have? I jumped into the stream and rescued the wayward shoe to the delight of my daughter. "Yay, you did it, Mommy!" she yelled. "Great job." Then she threw her other shoe in, too.

After I rescued the shoes and set them out to dry, I tried to decide if I was upset about the situation. At first, I was angry. I didn't want to be all wet. But I also didn't want to be angry. It really wasn't that big a deal.

Could I just go ahead and make the decision to laugh at myself and the world instead of getting upset about it? The situation was pretty ridiculous, after all. I must have looked quite preposterous chasing the shoes down the stream. So I went for it—I decided to stop being angry and laugh it off. Making our way back to the car to dry off, we left matching sloppy footprints and joked about how cold the water was. Laughing at myself was a lot easier than I thought it would be. It also made for a much more pleasant afternoon. Maybe just laughing it all off is the secret to happiness.

Grown-up Fun

In addition to the spontaneous fun with my family, I realized that I might benefit from doing my own fun thing, too. I started by trying to get the old trivia team back together, but we all decided that seven thirty was too late to go out, so no trivia for us old folks. Then I looked into an improv comedy class, but I couldn't find evening child care. I wanted to join a dodgeball league, but my husband strongly advised against it given my slow speed and poor throwing skills. I was asked to play hockey again, but the old women's league played only on Sunday mornings, which would mean trading in church for hockey. Hockey might have been more fun, but I still wasn't sure about that whole wrath thing. No need to take any risks of ending up in the belly of a whale for my disobedience, so I picked church over hockey. I joined a book club at the library, but it ended up disbanding over disagreements about whether to include books about zombies in the rotation (I was pro-zombie). Who knew finding fun was going to be so much work?

I didn't put a lot of time and energy into my search, though, mainly because I wasn't sure where I would be able to fit it into my schedule. I was already feeling overwhelmed with everything else I had going on—how would adding in one more thing make me happy? I didn't think it would. In fact, it kind of stressed me out. I realized that replacing something I didn't want to be doing with something enjoyable would probably make me happier. I just couldn't figure out how to do it. I wonder if part of the reason people aren't happy is that we simply don't know how to fit it into our schedules.

Fun as the Antidote

I remember listening to a speaker at a social work conference who said fun is the antidote to fear. He suggested that when clients are most aggressive and most afraid, that's the perfect time to make things fun and silly. It catches them off guard and allows for the fear to dissipate. He said laughter can overcome fear, sadness, and anger. As a therapist, I frequently took his advice, and noticed what a difference it could make with my clients. A quick joke or finding a way to catch them off guard often shifted difficult emotional situations into tolerable ones.

I began to wonder what would happen if I implemented this professional advice into my personal life, too. I decided that I would try to take on my bad moods with fun. I made a deal with myself that the next time I felt grumpy, I'd try to have fun, even if I didn't really want to. About a week later, the universe gave me a chance to practice. At the end of an unusually hard week, my daughter was invited to a birthday party. After the week I'd had, I just wanted to stay home and bury myself under the blankets. But my daughter loves parties, so I went. As we were driving there, my mind was racing, thinking about all the things I had to do and all the things I hadn't gotten done. I was feeling exhausted by the state of my life. The last thing I wanted to do was sit through a kid's birthday party. Or any party. I really just wanted to go home. After we arrived, my daughter invited me to join her in the bounce house, but I told her I really wasn't in the mood. Then I remembered my promise to myself and I did it anyway. I took off my shoes and climbed in. We jumped. We laughed. It was fun. I felt better. All that snarkiness I'd felt was suddenly gone. Just like that. I ate some cake, sang happy birthday, and even joined in on some of the party games. We ended up having a much better day than if I'd gone home and hidden under the blankets. In fact, we had a great day. Maybe fun really is the antidote.

Findings and Analysis

On the whole, I'd say that having fun made me happy. Having fun or being silly was the easiest way to get a happiness boost and change a bad mood. Adding in humor or playfulness made unpleasant tasks like working or putting my kid to bed far more enjoyable. Fun is kind of like that spoonful of sugar that makes the medicine go down.

However, I found that having fun took more work than I expected. When I made the effort to have fun, I was generally happier. I found that the more I had fun, the more it affected my mood even when I wasn't directly playing. The times when I felt the happiest over this year were when I was actively working on play. In fact, the month I was experimenting with fun was the best month of the year for me. Since I wasn't taking myself or the world so seriously, maybe my lighthearted-ness and humor just allowed me to see the problems differently, even if I did have to work at it a little bit.

I really do want fun to be part of my life, but I have to put it there. My happiness lies in my playfulness. For me, it really is the antidote to fear and anxiety, even if it's just for a few minutes. Other things get in the way, though, and I have to figure out how to prioritize fun rather than just trying to fit it in. I'm doing my best to make space for it. I've made it a goal to be as playful as I can and try to have some type of fun every day. It's easier said than done. Just to make sure I am honoring my commitment to myself, each night my daughter and I dance around the house singing the theme from a new commercial: "It's fun being weird, it's fun being weird, it's fun being weird, you should try it some-time." Best. Advice. Ever.

Chapter 9

The Health Nut

Area of Inquiry: Exercise and Nutrition

Methods:

- Plan meals for the week
- Develop healthier eating habits
- Start an exercise routine
- Make peace with my aging body
- Take care of lingering health issues

Happiness Quotient: 4/10

Experiment Design:

Given the power of fun, I wanted to find a way to carry that into my next experiment, which I decided would be health. I know you're thinking that health isn't fun, and I agree. Dentist appointments and mammograms are not fun. Eating salad is not fun. Lifting weights is not fun. So how could doing any of these things make me happier?

All the happiness literature touts the importance of exercise and nutrition. One happiness researcher refers to this as "vitality" and says it's needed to feel happy. The surgeon general says exercise is one of the things needed to achieve happiness. Within the mental health literature, the research around exercise and mood indicates a pretty strong link. Regular exercise has been demonstrated to be more effective in treating mild to moderate depression and anxiety than medications. There are also some findings now related to managing depression with probiotics and healthy eating. There must be something to all this, and I guess eating right and exercising do make our bodies feel better, but does that make us happy?

The research related to being healthier is pretty robust, but I also know from personal experience that exercise helps my mood. Before becoming a mom, I ran, I biked, I did yoga. I spent hours at the gym. Almost everything I did in my leisure time involved movement in some way. For me, exercise has always been fun and relaxing, so I was pretty confident that I'd find some happiness in taking on this experiment. I wasn't so sure about the healthy eating and doctors' appointments part, though. Regardless, I figured I would put the question to the test. Could making healthy changes to my lifestyle make me happier? I was about to find out.

Meals

I have a complicated relationship with food. I wish I didn't have to eat. I know, it's a little weird. But eating has become so confusing that I wish there was an easier way to nourish my body. I dream of a day when I can get all my needed calories and vitamins from a pill. If I were a real scientist, I'd develop that pill. Until that happens, one of my biggest challenges every day is deciding what to eat. What will taste good? What will make me feel good? What do I have in the house? I've worked with nutritionists and chefs to try to understand how to fuel my body, and I have a few standard meals I know I can eat. I end up eating the same thing every day, but it works for me. I do feel sorry for my husband, though.

To try to expand my repertoire, I went to the local health food store for ideas and inspiration. I didn't necessarily want to go gluten-free or eliminate free radicals or eat cricket protein flour (yes, that's a thing now) or get in on whatever other craze was hitting the shelves. I just wanted to find some good-tasting, nourishing food. How complicated could that be? As my daughter and I walked through the store and I considered all the options, I found out—*plenty* complicated. I came away more overwhelmed than inspired. We did get some food while we were there, though: cookies, popcorn, chips, and cupcakes. Since it came from the health food store, I'm going to count it as a healthy success.

Although I didn't get any great ideas about ways to eat healthier, I decided that I would at least try and be better about planning ahead and mixing up our meal options. Every Sunday, I planned the meals for the entire week. Although we had our "regulars," I also made an effort to try something new. Sometimes these were healthy options, like homemade soup. Sometimes we had one of our favorites, only modified to make them healthier, like turkey tacos. Sometimes I just said, "Who cares?" and we all had cereal and ice cream for dinner. Since I had a preschooler in the house, we also ate plenty of macaroni and cheese and goldfish crackers, but I added in applesauce or a slice of watermelon, too, just to be healthy.

We may not have been eating as healthy as we could have, but doing the meal planning helped to make eating a little less traumatic. Having the food in the house and a plan about what to eat saved us both time and the money it would have cost to eat out. While we didn't improve our diets much, I was less worried about what to eat, so I guess it did make me happier.

However, once the remodel of our home started, following the meal plan became a little more challenging. I often didn't have access to my kitchen or the power was sometimes turned off, making it hard to cook. We ended up eating out or picking up takeout a lot during that time. I also resorted to the cereal and ice cream dinner plan more often than I would have liked. Worst of all, once the remodel was done, I didn't revert back to my meal planning and shopping. The takeout was a lot easier (and tastier, too!) Alas, my experiment with healthy eating was short-lived. But I think most people's experiments with healthy eating are. Cake is just too delicious.

Exercise

My body likes to move. It always has. As a child, I wasn't the kid glued to the television. I was outside every chance I got. If you couldn't find me, I was probably in a tree or jumping over something with my bicycle. As an adult, I did what I could to keep this lifestyle going. I ran every day. When I got stuck in a desk job where I couldn't move around as freely, I began riding my bike to work so I could still get some physical activity in and some anxiety out. On my days off, I'd spend hours at the gym, taking multiple classes or going for a swim after my regular workout. I didn't do this to be healthy, I just really like to move. In fact, I was still Rollerblading up until my eighth month of pregnancy. After my daughter was born, I still found a way to fit active things in when I could. I did yoga with her crawling under me. We walked to the store, the library, and the park. At least once a week I'd walk the perimeter of the zoo, so she got to enjoy the animals and I got my workout in.

When I got sick, all that changed. I had to stop running when it became too painful. The stress and pain of the illness wore me out, so I was too exhausted to do any other kind of exercise. I was worried about pushing myself too hard and feared I would collapse from dehydration in the middle of the street. So I did nothing. In fact, even a walk to the park five blocks from our home seemed overwhelming.

When I picked this topic for one of my happiness experiments, I experienced the revelation that I hadn't worked out in a long time. When I'd started feeling better, I began doing short walks around my neighborhood, but I hadn't gotten my heart rate up or sweated in almost two years. I couldn't even remember the last time I'd done something that could be called a workout. Although my health was better now, I was still treating my body like it was fragile. I still feared what might happen if I pushed myself. Being so sedentary wasn't something that made me happy. I needed to do something different. It was time to take some chances and stop being afraid of my own body.

Knowing that exercise is something you just have to make up your mind to do, one morning I laced up my running shoes and I ran. I didn't run far or fast, but I ran. The next day, I ran a little farther and a little faster. I let my heart rate and breathing speed up without freaking out. I found that I wasn't afraid. In fact, I was having fun. I asked my body what it thought about running again and it screamed "yes!" in delight. I began running every morning again. I still don't go far, and I don't know that I'll ever run fast, but being able to move my body like this again has made me happy. A few weeks after restarting up my running routine, I noticed a difference in my mood. My husband noticed it, too. "I'm glad you're running again," he said one morning as I was singing while making breakfast. "That was always like the freedom for your soul." Truer words have never been spoken.

Once I realized that my body is a lot stronger than I thought it was, I added in a few different exercises. I went skiing a few times. I dusted off the Rollerblades. I filled my bike tires and took a few trips around the neighborhood. (Welcome back, old friends!) I went to a dance/exercise class offered by one of my neighbors. Although I wasn't really pushing myself as hard as I had before, at least I was doing something. Plus, it gave me an excuse to go buy some cool new exercise clothes. Are people still working out in leotards and leg warmers?

An Apple a Day Keeps the Doctors Away

Oddly, I eat apples almost every day and yet, I just couldn't avoid the doctor. As much as I didn't want to do any medical appointments, apples alone weren't cutting it. Initially, I didn't want to add anything into this experiment related to my medical health. I'd just spent the last two years hyper-focused on my body and health-related issues. I'd had my fill of doctors, appointments, tests, and worrying about my symptoms. But taking care of ourselves and doing preventive care can thwart potentially big health problems, so as a way to help make my future self happy, I decided to go ahead and do the routine care I needed. For example, I needed to get in to see the dentist. I'd also put off my "congratulations, now you're forty" mammogram for several years. I was pretty sure doing these things wouldn't make me happy, but it would be a relief, so I decided to just toss them in.

While I actively worked on my diet and exercise, I did not prioritize my medical appointments. Rather, I did my best to completely ignore them. I really didn't want to deal with it. However, the universe saw things differently and decided that since I had them on my list, I needed to get them done. At my annual check-up with my doctor, she found an abnormality in my breast. The mammogram was no longer a suggestion, it was now a requirement. The mammogram turned out to be normal and there were no ongoing concerns, but I don't know that I would have done it if the universe hadn't forced the issue. Similarly, the universe noticed I was avoiding the dentist. I'd developed a horrible TMJ disorder—a jaw condition, often caused by grinding and clenching of teeth at night, that can be very painful and cause a host of other problems, including headaches, muscle soreness, and vision issues. The symptoms got bad enough that I had to go to the dentist. It was no longer a choice. In the end, I was happy to cross "seeing the dentist" and "getting a mammogram" off the list, but it was not really in the way I wanted. Guess that's just the way the universe works sometimes. Thanks, universe... I think.

Finding Peace with an Aging Body

I was standing in line at the grocery store one morning, eavesdropping on a conversation between two women. Upon being asked how she was feeling, the women commented, "I'm okay, usual aches and pains, you know. If I get up and something isn't hurting, I wonder if I died." They both laughed and went on to joke about how their physical ailments seemed to be the main topic of any conversation. They reminisced about times when catching up with friends and family were about topics other than blood pressure and bowel movements.

I laughed in my head, but I also thought about how the conversations with my friends had shifted in recent years. I'd recently talked with an old friend who told me about his health struggles related to developing diabetes. I met another friend for dinner who shared that he'd recently had an ER visit for what he believed to be a heart attack. And the primary topic of conversation with another of my friends was her recent knee replacement. "How are you feeling?" has become the opening line in many more of my conversations than I ever expected. Although I am used to this among my parents' generation, have my friends and I really reached this stage in our lives? When did we get old?

When I became sick, I began to treat my body with kid gloves. Every little bump, bruise, ache, or strange feeling sent me into a complete panic. I was certain I was going to die any time my muscles got a little sore or I sneezed too many times. Any unusual body sensation sent me running to Dr. Google to learn of the many possible diseases that were surely going to end me. However, as my doctor, my friends, my therapist, and the ladies in the grocery store pointed out to me, we all get older. When we get older, bodies break down and sometimes ache. Things don't work as well as they used to. That's why NFL players retire at thirty-two and why there are age categories in marathons. Medical advances keep us alive a lot longer, but that doesn't stop the aging process. The band R.E.M. was right—everybody does hurt sometimes.

I somehow had to accept that my body was getting older. We don't get to keep our twenty-year-old bodies. As I age, I'm probably going to have more health problems, more aches, more times when I don't feel great. That's all completely normal, and I needed to figure out how to accept it. I wanted to fall in love with my body. I wanted to be grateful for all it can do, not worry about how time is ticking. I wanted to be okay with the aches and pains and old-person limitations. Lamenting the state it was in wasn't making me happy.

I decided the best way to approach the problem was to be grateful. I realized that I was very lucky in all that my body could do. I began to say thank you instead of searching for all that might be wrong. I stopped looking up medical ailments online and even blocked WebMD and wrongdiagnosis.com from my browser. I followed my doctors' recommendations and stopped trying to fight the process. I let my body just be. Eventually, we were able to become friends again, growing old together. I still have to remind myself of that when these aches and pains show up, but it feels a little easier now. Making peace with my body has made me very happy.

Findings and Analysis

Did changing my eating and exercise habits make me happier? Not really. Maybe a little. I was excited to be exercising again and think it improved my mood, and planning meals helped me to feel more organized, but it didn't really improve the quality of the food we were eating. I think my daughter had marshmallows for breakfast today. Not in her cereal, just marshmallows.

Reality is, I didn't work on this experiment very hard. I did exercise, but I did only things that I like and find to be fun. I didn't do any of the exercises that are necessary but not enjoyable to me, like weights and interval training. So I can't even really say I exercised. I had fun.

I didn't try very hard with the food either. Though I threw in some extra salads and made some healthy substitutions in old favorite recipes, I usually had a cookie chaser. I don't know if being healthier leads to being happier, but the experts say it does, so I'll believe it. I just don't want to do the work myself to find out. ***America nods head in agreement***

One thing I'm sure of, though, is that during the times when I was dealing with my illness and not feeling healthy, I wasn't happy. I had to accept the fact that my body is where I live and I need to tend to it. Although exercise, eating better, and going to my doctors' appointments aren't directly related to my happiness, if they keep me healthy and make my body feel good, they're probably worth doing to avoid future misery. I guess the hard part is that even if I do all this, I am still going to have aches and pains. That's just what happens to aging bodies.

All in all, although sweating is painful, eating cauliflower and quinoa is agony, and going to the dentist is torture, it may all be worth it for the sake of long-term happiness. On the other hand, my experimentation wasn't exactly sufficient to show with any certainty that it's better to take the short-term pain of healthy eating and exercise than to go for the instant gratification of eating pizza in front of the TV. I think I'll experiment a little more with the pizza-and-TV thing and let you know.

Chapter 10

In Service of Others

Area of Inquiry: Volunteer work

Methods:

- Make time and space for service
- Reconnect with the previous volunteer sites
- Become more active in my church
- Volunteer at my daughter's school
- Crochet hats for the homeless

Happiness Quotient: 10/10

Experiment Design:

This is an experiment I'd been looking forward to since the start of the project. In my life, I've always been happiest when I'm serving others. I feel more like myself than at any other time. It provides me meaning. It provides happiness. So much so that helping others became my vocation and profession.

The research behind volunteering indicates a positive link. Even as early as ancient times, the benefits of altruism were well-known. Aristotle said helping others is the way to individual well-being. Current day research shows that service and compassion are linked with both immediate mood boosts and long-term happiness. There are several studies indicating that those who volunteer regularly are more satisfied with their lives than those who don't.

Since becoming a researcher, I hadn't done any direct client contact in some time. I was excited about the chance to get back into working with people directly. I wanted to serve. I needed to serve. I needed to be with others and connect in those broken and vulnerable places, not only for their benefit but for mine.

However, I had this problem. I had a job. I had a daughter. I was busy trying to have fun, meditate, and plan out meals. I had other things that required my attention. Finding the time and energy to serve others was difficult. I already knew that volunteering would make me happy, but could I find a way to do it? Could I make space for the thing that I knew would create happiness?

Service History

I found the joy of volunteering in college. (I guess that's expected when one attends a school whose motto is "Men and Women in Service of Others.") The first semester of my freshman year was intense for lots of reasons, and when I returned for second semester, I was a little broken and very exhausted. One of my courses threw me a lifeline in the form of a service learning option. Being an overachiever, I agreed to take it on, and I ended up working at a hospice for men with AIDS. How I ended up there is another story, but it was clearly the place for me to be. Once a week, I would go to this house and "help out." I mowed the lawn. I painted. I ran errands. I had discussions about the meaning of life. I dusted. I made ice cream sundaes. I listened to regrets and fears. I cried with them. I don't really know how much "help" I was, but for the first time in my life, I understood what it means to be a human. I connected with people on a completely different level and saw how much we must rely on each other to make it through this crazy world. Others' vulnerability allowed me to be vulnerable, too. In my sitting with these men, full of vulnerability and love, I saw how the Holy Spirit works through our brokenness. I felt compassion and gratitude. I learned about hope and resilience. That weekly outing became more than a reprieve from my college stress or extra points on my final grade, it provided me a way to heal, to love, and to grow. After that experience, service became more than just a college buzzword. It became my calling and purpose.

In the twenty years since, service has provided me with a way to be with others, a way to get out of my own head, and a way to feel like I'm making some sort of difference in the world. I've volunteered in a variety of settings and among different populations. It has been the one constant that makes me feel connected, makes me feel human, and can make me feel better regardless of what else is going on in my life.

However, after my daughter was born, much like other things in my life, volunteering became more challenging. I tried to find organizations where I could take her with me or where we could volunteer together, but oddly enough, most places didn't really need a toddler's help. My service to the community ended up taking a backseat.

When my daughter started preschool, I began volunteering at an assisted-living community. It was by far the best two hours of my week. The residents provided me with laughter and fun. I helped them paint pictures and read stories to them. Seemed like a good trade. When I went back to work full time, I stopped going. As much as I wanted to go paint and read, there just didn't seem to be time. I knew this work was important to me, so I had to find a way to fit it into my schedule. But how?

Making Space

The first step before committing to any service project was to make room for it. When I took this goal on, I was working from home one day a week, and I figured I'd try to fit something in between my project work and phone calls. I blocked out a few hours for it on my calendar.

Now I just needed to decide what I wanted to do. I started by contacting the mental health association I'd worked with previously. I was told its process had changed, so I'd have to go in and meet with someone, do a new orientation, and interview with different sites. When I checked my schedule, I saw that my calendar was filled with meetings and appointments for the next three weeks, even during my so-called reserved time. I guess this wouldn't be the place.

Okay, so how about doing something intermittent without having to make a commitment? I asked about volunteering at my daughter's school, and the teacher told me there wasn't a lot of need during the summer months. When the regular schedule resumed in the fall, there would be the opportunity to come in and teach some social skills to the kids. It wasn't immediate, but at least I had a plan in place.

In the meantime, I really wanted to return to the assisted-living facility where I'd previously volunteered. I missed the residents. I contacted the facility and was told it would be okay for me to just come in whenever I could. I got an activities calendar and decided to go on Sunday afternoons, but family commitments ended up getting in the way. Then I planned to go in late to work a couple of times a month, but something important always seemed to come up. Then I planned to help out with a couple of the facility's one-time events, but the weather was bad or I was too tired or there was something good on TV. I ended up with a lot of excuses and not very much action. As much as I wanted to go, I never made it back.

Then I was asked to join a committee at church. Finally, here was something I could do! I could easily spare an hour after church one Sunday a month to help plan some church activities. But the meetings ended up being moved to the middle of the week, and I had to sneak out of work for a long lunch in order to make the meetings. This plan wasn't working either.

By the end of the month, I'd determined that I probably couldn't take on any regular volunteer commitments. I didn't want to give up on this experiment yet, though, so I decided on another plan. In the evenings, I'd crochet hats and scarves for people who needed them, and by winter I'd have enough to drop off at the homeless shelter. It was a way to contribute that didn't require leaving my living room. Perfect.

As November rolled around, I'd crocheted a grand total of three hats and a scarf. Does three hats and a scarf count as service?

No Service Sadness

Let's do a quick review of my service experiment:

crickets chirping

Yes, initially, this experiment was kind of a bust. It wasn't that I didn't have good intentions. Life just got in the way. It seems to do that.

I know serving makes me happy. It always has. I would say that in the past, it was one of the biggest factors in my overall contentment. The fact that I couldn't do it now made me sad. I clearly needed to shift priorities, I just didn't know how. Like the goal of achieving a work/life balance, not being able to do the things that I knew would make me happy created an internal crisis for me. Why was I spending so much of my time and energy on things I didn't care about and sacrificing the important things in return? If I wanted to be happy, I needed to find space for the things that mattered. Service mattered. I had to demonstrate to myself that it was important enough to put into my life.

I think many of us come to a space in our lives where we have to figure out what really matters. I knew what would make me happy, yet I didn't choose it. Why not? I think the answer to this question is actually the secret to happiness (or lack thereof). Why don't we choose happiness?

I don't know the answer. I wish I did. I know that for me it was a very complex issue. I had a lot of shoulds: "I should be working," "I should be spending time with my child," "I should take care of my own house before helping someone else out with theirs," "I have plenty of my own problems, so I should deal with my own crap first." These were excuses, not reasons. I was choosing overthinking and obligations. I wasn't choosing happiness.

If I really wanted to give happiness a chance in my life, I had to make a decision. I didn't want to throw this experiment out, believing I had no positive findings. I just needed to rework it a little.

Making Space, Take 2

If I really was serious about service, maybe I should just throw myself into it. Why not simply run away from all my responsibilities and go join a convent or a Buddhist monastery or the Peace Corps or something of the sort? Then I could just do service all the time. As much as I would still love to do that (and it may just happen), I knew that wasn't realistic for my life at this point.

Instead, I was going to have to be creative with service. I had the thought that maybe I could find a way to do service with something I was already doing, kind of a two-for-one special. I know it's not really prioritizing, but my other attempts at service hadn't worked. Maybe this could be an innovative way to still be true to my values without ignoring my obligations.

My first attempt at the two-for-one was at the church. I agreed to teach the kids' Sunday school. I was already at church anyway, my daughter could join me, and it wasn't going to take a lot of extra time, so that was a place to start. Initially, it was pretty great. I had fun with the kids and felt useful. I was teaching about once a month, taking turns with other members of the congregation. As other people dropped out of teaching due to their own obligations, much of it fell to me and I was eventually teaching every week. That meant I had to miss the sermon every week. I decided I wasn't willing to make that trade. This two-for-one didn't work.

However, that didn't mean I couldn't do anything for the church. The pastor said she needed help with the website and Facebook page, and that was something I could do at any time. I didn't have to miss work or find childcare, so I agreed to take it on. I redesigned the website, set up a place for members to post photos, and updated the Facebook page every week. The work required me to interact with a lot of church members and learn more about the church's services and activities. The more involved I became, the more connected I felt to my church, the pastor, and the congregation. I was not only providing a desperately needed service, I was also building connections and a community. It wasn't exactly what I'd had in mind, but it was a way I could serve without feeling guilty for ducking out of my other commitments.

As for the two-for-one deal, I had another idea. I was teaching the Mental Health Interventions with Children course at the university, and I wondered what would happen if I held one of my classes at my daughter's preschool. It would give my students a chance to do some hands-on work with actual children while giving the preschoolers an opportunity to learn some new skills. The graduate students developed and presented fun activities for the preschoolers. It went well and we all had a good time. Win-win.

At the same time, though, it felt like a cop-out. If I really wanted to do service, I needed to make the time for it. I wasn't choosing happiness, I was trying to fit it in. I had to make a decision about what was important. So I did. I blocked out my calendar (for real this time). It meant working later in the evenings, but I didn't care. Instead of going into work, I spent every Wednesday morning with the preschool students, teaching them about making friends, managing emotions, and solving problems. I taught them some mindfulness activities and did meditation with them. It was the best part of my week. I'd made the right choice.

I continued to volunteer regularly at my daughter's school and at the church, where I still maintain the Facebook page and website. I even helped to organize a Bible study. I never made it back to the assisted-living facility, but I'm hoping to do so one day. And I'm still working on the crocheting project for the homeless, though it's coming along slowly. I've added another hat to my collection, and I'm working on the matching scarf. Maybe by next winter.

Findings and Analysis

I knew that recommitting myself to service would make me happy. The research says it will, and it has before. Serving others and being with a community were things I wanted in my life. I just needed to make them a priority. I wasn't making the time for them. I put other things in front of service. I let other people dictate what was important. I had to make the decision to choose my own happy, even at the risk of giving things up or letting others down.

Although it took me some time and creativity to test out my experiment of serving others, once I did I remembered why it's so important for my happiness. It's who I am. It's how I connect. It's where I find meaning. It's where I get to see the Holy Spirit at work. It's so much bigger than happy. A part of me thinks that service alone could probably bring complete happiness.

This experiment reminded me of other things, too. It reminded me that I get to choose what I do with my time. It reminded me that I am in control of my happy. It helped me prioritize what really matters: a commitment to my community, being with others makes, feeling like I'm part of something bigger than myself. Through service, I get a chance to bring light to darkness and heal my own wounds. I get to help others find their happy. Which in turn makes me happy. Hmm… maybe I shouldn't rule out the convent or Peace Corps just yet.

Chapter 11

The Tribe

Area of Inquiry: Relationships

Methods:

- Rekindle old friendships and start new ones
- Ask for and receive help
- Share the parenting
- Participate in regular activities with other people
- Make time for my marriage
- Spend time with family

Happiness Quotient: 10/10

Experiment Design:

I recently came across an interesting article about happiness around the world. Happiness looks different in other cultures, but there was one commonality in every nation: having friends and family around. Humans are social beings and we need to be connected. I would agree.

The times in my life when I've been the happiest are when I've had regular and meaningful contact with people I care about and enjoy spending time with.

The research is pretty clear about relationships' importance to happiness. In fact, close relationships have been cited as the single most important factor in happiness. Conversely, loneliness has been indicated to be one of the primary factors in both poor mental and physical health. There was recently a *New York Times* article about how loneliness is becoming a public health crisis. Loneliness isn't just unpleasant—it's actually killing us.

I believe this is because having others around us isn't just nice but also a biological imperative. Our ancient ancestors understood the importance of having a tribe. Humans are pack animals; we need each other to survive. We need to reproduce and keep those offspring alive. We need others for safety, security, and shared resources. While there have been quite a few changes in how we find safety and get access to resources since caveman times, our need for each other hasn't changed. It's still part of our DNA. We find happiness in being around others so that we'll seek others out to be in our pack. Evolution is tricky like that.

Researchers, happiness authors, therapists, pastors, bartenders, and executives at the greeting-card companies all agree: We need each other. There is some debate, however, as to the best way to approach this. As a society, we've come up with a lot of unique ways to interact with each other. With a click of a button, we can find hundreds of "friends" and "followers." Thanks to technology, we can talk to others immediately regardless of location. We can call, text, and even see the faces of our loved ones using programs like FaceTime and Skype. In fact, we can connect with the entire world without ever leaving our homes. The research has yet to determine whether this type of communication and interaction is a good thing for us and our relationships.

Despite the fact that we're more connected than ever, we're also lonelier. All these advances in technology have created some distance because they also provide new opportunities for mobility. Unlike in caveman days (or even sixty years ago), we move away from our families. Friends grow up and leave town. We connect on Facebook, but aren't necessarily spending time together or sharing our resources. On one of my harder parenting days, I asked my mom how my grandmother had managed to be so happy and content in her role as a stay-at-home mom. "She didn't have to do it alone," she replied. Her parents and siblings (as well as in-laws) were all in the same town. She knew all her neighbors. She had the same friends for years and years. She had people to share her joy, and they were happy. She had a tribe.

I realized that a tribe was something I was missing. After my daughter was born, I learned that what they say is true, it does take a village. Biologically, I wasn't meant to do this alone. While my husband and I could typically manage the ins and outs of parenting tasks, I still needed people around me to make me laugh, to hold my child for a minute, to give me a shoulder to cry on. I needed more than a sad-face emoji and a virtual hug. I needed a tribe. I figured this experiment would give me a great chance to build one and see for myself how relationships affect happiness.

Relationships

I'm pretty lucky. I have good relationships in general. I get along really well with my parents, in-laws, aunts, uncles, and cousins. My siblings are my best friends. I'm lucky to have a nice extended family. The only problem is that most of them live really far away. That makes it hard for them to watch my child or go for a hike with me. Hugs are pretty much out of the question. I've also never had problems making friends. I have lots of friends with diverse interests who have provided a source of fun, a place to vent my feelings, and help with moving, as long I've provided the beer and pizza. However, friendships have seasons. In high school and college, my friends and I were in it together, through good, bad, hilarious, stupid, and tumultuous. They truly were my village. But as I moved from college into young adulthood, my college friends moved away and I created a new tribe. It was a group of people to hang with, spend holidays with, complain about work with, and have fun with. Over time, though, many of these people moved on with their lives, too—new jobs, kids, etc. Over the past few years, my tribe has spread out across the entire world and has a whole new set of obligations and commitments. If I moved now, I'd have to hire professional movers who won't work for just pizza.

After I had my daughter, I didn't have regular contact with anyone other than my family and the pediatrician. Sadly, having kids is surprisingly lonely. I didn't have a true tribe anymore. While my parents and my husband helped with my daughter, I was missing the other things my old relationships provided, like laughter, companionship, fun, and emotional support. Parenting requires a lot of "nurturing energy" to keep that little life going, and often, there's not a lot of energy for anyone else. As a parent, it's easy to be consumed by the day-to-day routine. Mere existence becomes exhausting. The idea of visiting relatives or making plans to be with friends isn't just overwhelming, it's also a logistical challenge. Basically, these are your options:

Option #1 – Bring the kids along. In some cases this might work, but it's often more trouble than it's worth. Ever tried to catch up on gossip and drink wine while simultaneously attempting to prevent your little one from eating spaghetti off a stranger's plate?

Options #2 – Arrange for a babysitter. ***laughs hysterically*** Seriously, finding a trustworthy babysitter is a lot harder than you'd think.

Option #3 – Set up a playdate. Getting together with other moms is great. The little ones can destroy the house and no one cares. However, what in my day amounted to simply asking, "Can Amy come out and play?" now requires hours of planning. It's fun to get together, but it also means working around multiple parties' nap times, school schedules, soccer games, illnesses, and all those other things that kept you in the house with your own kid, only multiplied. The scheduling becomes overwhelming, almost to the point where a few minutes of adult interaction isn't worth the hassle.

Option #4 – Stay at home in yoga pants watching *Handy Manny* for the eight hundredth time. Though Manny didn't provide a lot of friendship and support, he did entertain my daughter enough that I could scroll through Twitter a time or two to find out what all my friends were doing.

Unfortunately, thanks to these limited options, I'd lost a lot of my tribe just when I needed it the most. I knew it was time to get it back, but how?

One Is Silver, the Other Is Gold

I figured that an easy way to start was to try to rekindle old relationships. Although I hadn't been in contact with certain friends for many years, I figured we could just pick up where we left off. Luckily, because of Facebook, locating and communicating with old friends was pretty easy. Some responded. Some were happy to say hello, but weren't interested in getting together. Some wanted to catch up in person, but couldn't find the time. Some never responded. As I said, friendships have seasons.

Eventually, I was able to get together in person with some of them. A bunch of us even got together for a mini friendship retreat. But we're all busy. Work deadlines, dirty diapers, and family commitments tended to get in the way of further gatherings. But while I wasn't spending much face time with them, I did feel more supported. I felt comfortable reaching out via text for a laugh or a cry and the promise of an eventual lunch or something. It made me feel like I wasn't completely alone. It was a start.

Relying on my old friends wasn't the only option, though. I could make new friends. It's like that old song: "Make new friends, but keep the old. One is silver and the other is gold." But I couldn't just find them on the elementary school playground or in the college dorm anymore. Unfortunately, at this season in my life, making new friends might take work. If I was going to make new friends, how would I do it?

The literature around friendship indicates that building relationships requires two main things: repeated exposure and shared interests. Where was I spending time with the same people where we had similar interests? My first thought was church. I see most of the members at least once a week. But similar interests turned out to be another matter. I soon found that we didn't have much else in common beyond church. Most of the congregation is significantly older and eighty-year-olds aren't often up for going Rollerblading with me. They're a great source of emotional support and I finally got my hugs, but I needed to keep looking for people who could meet some of my other needs, like having some fun.

I tried to make friends at work, and this also wasn't a raving success. I saw them often, but we didn't really have similar interests. And when I was done with my workday, I didn't want to spend more time thinking or talking about work. I was able to find a small group of people to eat lunch with, but I don't know that I would really say I made friends.

Repeated exposure wasn't working, so I focused on the similar interests thing instead. Figuring I'd try to connect with other moms, I went to story time at the library, chatted up other moms at the park, and began saying hello to all the other parents at my daughter's school. This provided me with moments of interaction, but I wouldn't say that I made any actual friends this way either. While interests were the same, I didn't necessarily have repeated contact with them. Most of the encounters resulted in a single fun but brief interaction, kind of like one-night stands of parenting playdates.

I didn't want one-night stands. I was in this for relationships. I tried doing parenting meet-ups, I joined a parenting class, and I attended parenting events in the community. While many of these led nowhere, eventually I found a match. I saw a notice for a regular neighborhood play group posted on Facebook, and while I was somewhat hesitant, I figured that if nothing else, my daughter would wear herself out playing with the other kids and take a nice long nap afterward. The first group turned out to be better than I expected, so we began attending regularly. My daughter napped after each group and I met some really great people. We even had similar interests beyond parenting. I'd made some friends. It felt nice.

As my friendships grew and I became better-connected with others, I began to feel happier. It was so great to laugh, hug, share gossip and snacks, and just be around other people. I began to notice that any time I was with others, I didn't worry about whether or not I was happy. I was able to just enjoy and be present, which is what happiness is all about.

Date Nights

While I was enjoying both my old and new friendships, I didn't want to ignore my most important relationships. I didn't think I needed to work on my relationship with my daughter—she already got a lot of my time and energy—but I figured I should pay some attention to my husband. He'd also kind of had to take a backseat once our little one arrived. It happens.

I had some great plans for rekindling our relationship. We'd have regular date nights, do fun things together, and even go on weekend getaways. I had good intentions, but my plans never came to fruition. Like with my friends, things got in the way. Work problems, exhaustion, lack of a babysitter, and football season all pushed date nights to the side. I think we went to one matinee while our daughter attended a birthday party. I'm counting it.

Even though things didn't work out as planned, I didn't stress too much about not spending more time on this portion of my experiment. As a whole, our relationship is good. We're kind to each other. We communicate well. We enjoy each other's company. We like parenting together. I still wouldn't mind that weekend getaway, but I'll take what I can get. For now, that's a Netflix binge and takeout pizza until we both fall asleep on the couch. Yep, it's the perfect relationship.

Asking for Help

Although part of my intent in building up my tribe was to have fun, I knew there were other benefits to having a good support system. The evolutionary reason for a tribe is so that we can help each other out. The current term is *social capital*, which basically means you're nice to others so they'll do nice things for you in return. While I'm happy to help anyone out in a pinch, I'm not that great at asking for help. I think it's because I don't want anyone to see me as needing help. I don't want anyone to think that I'm not strong or that I can't handle it or that I can't do it on my own. I don't want anyone to see that I might be vulnerable or, even worse, broken.

Intellectually, I know we need to have other people around us especially when we're broken. I base this on the many nature documentaries I've seen. In the animal kingdom, creatures are most at risk when they've just given birth, when they're nursing or simply have young with them, and when they're sick or injured. Animals that are part of a pack let their pack help them during these times of vulnerability. They let the other animals protect them and provide them food. Animals that aren't part of a pack hide until their bodies have healed. My instincts have been to hide when I'm vulnerable, but since humans are pack animals, maybe there's a better option for me. Maybe I could learn something from the animals.

If I truly wanted to understand the connection between relationships and happiness, I needed to give myself a chance to benefit from support that having strong relationships could provide. Luckily for me, the universe agreed and offered me some opportunities to practice.

Lesson #1 – The Kidney Stone

Late last summer I developed a kidney stone. A horrible, painful, silly kidney stone. It hurt. A lot. Eventually, I needed to get help because I didn't know what was going on. I only knew I was in a lot of pain. However, I had some dilemmas. I was home alone with my daughter. It was 7:30 at night, which is too late to call on a friend or a neighbor for help. They'd already be sleeping or at least have their pajamas on and be thinking about sleeping, I was sure.

My husband was on the other side of town, so I figured I'd just wait for him. But the pain kept getting worse and he wasn't answering his phone. I figured I could get myself to the hospital, but what would I do with my daughter? I didn't want her to have to sit in the ER with me. Suddenly, all those fears I had as a mom of a youngster were coming true. I was in pain, I needed help, I needed someone to care for her, and I didn't know what to do.

Eventually, I relented. My desire to be a superhero was no match for my kidney stone. It seriously felt like kryptonite in my body. Even though it was, like, the middle of the night (8:15 p.m., to be exact), I called my parents. I asked for help and apologized for doing so. Their response? "We love you. We will help you. And it's really not that late. We don't even have our pajamas on yet." My parents took my child, and my husband came to the ER and held my hand because he wanted to be there. I told him several times he could go home and get some sleep so that he could go to work the next day (by this time it was nearly 10:00 at night, much too late for anyone to be up), but he said no. He loved me and wanted to make sure I was okay.

That night, I received great gifts of love from those most important to me. I fought it, but I didn't have a choice. They were going to love me and take care of me whether I wanted them to or not.

I guess the universe didn't find my efforts to accept love from others to be sufficient, because it allowed me to try again. My kidney stone didn't pass, which meant more invasive procedures, which meant anesthesia, which meant working out days off and childcare during my recovery. So, I bucked up and made childcare arrangements with a friend and asked my co-worker to cover a meeting for me.

However, the day after my surgery, I did exactly the opposite of what would have been useful. I went to work. I didn't want to inconvenience clients or make my boss pick up the slack. Instead, I drove my kid to my parents' house so they wouldn't have to come get her. When we got home, I played Pokémon with her and went for a walk when what I really wanted was just to cuddle up in my bed. I felt like crap most of the day but fought through it so as not to bother others or appear as if I couldn't handle it. Take that, universe. You can't tell me what to do!

Oh, but it can. Lucky for me, I got the chance to practice again.

Lesson #2 – Helping Mom

Later in the fall, my mom had some medical issues. She ended up in the hospital for about a week, culminating in surgery and recovery. It was a challenging time for my family. My mom was being well cared for by the doctors, but there was still a lot to think about. I needed to make sure my dad was eating and sleeping. I needed to keep my brother and sister updated. I needed to make sure my parents were amused while hanging out in the hospital and didn't get too scared or too bored or whatever. I wanted to help out in any way I could.

Having learned some lessons from my surgery, I called work and said I wasn't going to be in. I was taking the entire week off. I asked my boss to handle some things and didn't feel even a little bit guilty about it. And when one of my friends offered to pick up my daughter after school to give me more time at the hospital, I gratefully accepted the help.

After my mom went home, she needed some recovery time. I went back to work at this point, but I'd go over in the evenings and on weekends to help with laundry and make sure my parents had meals to eat. I was running myself a little ragged. I was working hard to catch up at work, prepare for the class I was teaching, take care of my parents, take care of my child, and plan for a perfect Thanksgiving. Ultimately, it was too much and I fell apart a little bit. I was so worried about taking care of others that I forgot to take care of myself. I realized that I couldn't do it all and I certainly couldn't do it alone. I decided to make some changes. I asked for help. I called my aunt and she was able to help with my parents. I called my sister and she was able to help with Thanksgiving. I asked a co-worker to take over a project so I wouldn't have to push myself to meet the deadline. I asked a neighbor to watch my daughter so I could grade finals from the class I was teaching. My mother-in-law came and helped me get caught up on my own laundry. I asked a friend to meditate with me and asked my church to pray for me. Everyone was more than happy to help me because that's what tribes do.

I heard you, universe. Time to slow down. Time to make some changes. Time to let myself love and be loved, even if it meant inconveniencing others. I think I did a better job this time, but only after having a breakdown. I was getting close, but the universe wanted to give me one more try.

Lesson #3 – Stitches

On the night of my daughter's Christmas program at school, I was making dinner and trying to get everything ready. My parents, my aunt, and my mother-in-law were all on their way to join us for an evening of adorably sung Christmas carols. Because I was doing several things at once, I wasn't really paying attention and sliced my finger open on a can of soup. I tried to keep making dinner, but I kept bleeding. As hard as I tried to get my blood to coagulate, it just wasn't paying attention. I was going to have to get stitches. Great.

But unlike the other times when I'd needed help, I didn't fight it. I asked my mother-in-law to finish dinner. I asked my mom to get my child dressed for the program. I asked my aunt to take pictures and my husband to send my regrets to the teacher. I asked my father to drive me to urgent care. And I got stitches in my hand.

The following day, I rested. I was supposed to volunteer at the Christmas party at my child's school, but I canceled. I felt like it was an inconvenience, but her teacher understood. Not only was her teacher not angry, the children in the class told me they had said a prayer for my finger to heal. Rather than pushing myself, I decided to take care of myself. I went to my parents' house and let my mom bake cookies with my daughter while I took a nap. The next day, my neighbor offered to shovel my sidewalk. Since I couldn't get a glove on or hold a shovel, I happily accepted. This time, I just let people help me. I got it now, universe. I promise.

Findings and Analysis

The happiness literature is right—we need to have other people around us. At least I do. Being around other people provided a beautiful reprieve from my own thoughts. While I preferred face-to-face interactions, even something as simple as a text from my sister often brought me an instant happiness boost. This experiment was about more than just having a laugh or getting a hug, though. It also showed me I don't have to do this alone. I don't have to navigate this really hard and difficult world by myself. I have a whole team of people to guide me, support me, encourage me, and carry some of the burden when I can't do it by myself anymore. That's what we're supposed to do. Evolution says so.

Like the other experiments, I had to work at it at first. I had to acknowledge how lonely I was. Then I had to take steps to fix the problem. I had to let go of preconceived notions about friendships. I had to make the time and effort to reach out to others. I had to accept that rejection often didn't have anything to do with me but with the busy lives we all lead. I had to accept that many of us, myself included, didn't have the time to hang out and be present with each other the way we did back in the college dorm. To make this work, I had to intentionally make the time and effort for relationships and prioritize them. However, even if I made the time, the other person had to as well. This kind of coordination often proves tricky, which is why too many of us end up on the couch in yoga pants instead of spending time with others.

To get the full benefit of relationship happiness, I also had to do less. I had to stop making relationships one-sided by feeling like I had to take care of others. I could also let people help me. I had to get out of the way and let my friends and family do what friends and family do. Learning to trust and rely on others made me less fearful. Although it took a couple of tries, I'm appreciative that the universe helped me learn this lesson and reminded me that people have my back. I don't need to worry so much, which makes me really happy.

While I don't have all the answers about happiness, this is one I can feel pretty confident about. Be around other people. This may mean that you have to make some choices. You may need to cut out some of the things you don't really need to do to make room for actual face-to-face time with other people. I would argue that it's well worth the effort. Being around others is what we're biologically programmed to do. We should listen to evolution on this one. Unlike the narwhal, mudskipper or giraffe weevil,[4] I think evolution got this one right.

---

4 Twenty Weird Animals that Prove Evolution was Drunk (2014). https://www.buzzfeed.com/kellyoakes/the-weirdest-animals-on-earth?utm_term=.nqwygMlPZ9#.ruMYZw4B27

Chapter 12

Being Bold

Area of Inquiry: Adventure

Methods:

- Try new things
- Create a bucket list
- Stop being afraid
- Eat new foods
- Say yes to adventure
- Make mistakes

Happiness Quotient: 7/10

Experiment Design:

While working on this project, I heard a great song on the radio: "Brand New," by Ben Rector. It has a line that really resonated with me: "I feel like taking chances, like making big mistakes." I wanted to be braver. I wanted to try new things. I wanted to make some mistakes.

I was ready to stop being so afraid and worrying about everything. If I was to find happiness, I'd need to be bolder about it. It was time to reclaim my adventurous spirit.

Although somewhat limited in the research, there is some evidence that being adventurous is related to happiness. It appears as though happy people worry less and have less fear. There are some mood benefits from adrenaline rushes and feelings of confidence that result from facing a fear. There is also some indication that those with more adventurous personality types tend to be happier, but I am not sure which way this correlation works. Are happy people more adventurous, or does adventure bring about happiness? It's hard to determine the cause and effect, but if nothing else, people who are having adventures are out there living life. Isn't that part of what happiness is all about? Why not find out?

Excellent Adventures

Part of my awesome has been my sense of adventure. For most of my life, I was the person who was "up for anything." I wasn't afraid. I was fearless. I was bold. I loved experiencing everything life had to offer, and people are often surprised by my variety of interests. I played hockey, I have a stand-up comedy routine, I participated in a stair climbing competition (forty-six flights!), and I jumped off a boat into a shark-infested lagoon in Mexico.[5] I was always learning or trying something new. It was more than fun, it was awesome.

Then I became a mom. Suddenly, everything was scary. I didn't want to do anything but shelter my child. Sure, we went to the park and the zoo, but beyond that, we have lived a very safe life. Even as she gets older and starts taking chances, I don't. I've gotten stuck.

Recently, a friend started a bucket list group where we support each other's dreams. When it was my turn to state my goals, I didn't know what to say. I couldn't think of what kind of daring or interesting things I'd like to do. I said that I'd like to see Machu Picchu someday,

---

5 And by sharks, I mean little, tiny fish, but basically the same thing.

but I don't have any plans to go there. In fact, I don't have any plans for the future. I don't even have plans for next week. And without goals, there's no place for hope. We all need something to dream about. One of my first goals was to create a bucket list. Whether or not I do the things on the list, I figured it would serve as a reminder that there's still a lot of life left to live.

Fighting Fear

Although I'm fun and adventurous, I'm also a worrier. I am an overthinker. My brain likes analyzing and thinking so much that it will come up with solutions to problems that don't exist and new solutions to problems that have already been solved. I tend to worry about a lot of things, things that other people never even consider. I pretty much have contingency plans for anything that could possibly happen. Have a completely unrealistic problem you need someone to handle? I'm your girl!

While my thought patterns are sometimes amusing, they can also be quite annoying. My worrying tends to get in the way of a lot of things. It is a major barrier to my happiness. I decided that one thing I would need to do to be bold is to let go of fear. I needed to say good-bye to worrying. I needed to be braver.

There are lots of therapeutic techniques for dealing with fear, and I've pretty much tried them all. I used cognitive behavior therapy techniques to get into logical arguments with my fears and try to prove them wrong. Fears are pretty smart, though. They outwitted even my best arguments. I used exposure therapy techniques to play the fears out as far as they would go and let myself experience all the possible outcomes of whatever I was trying to solve. I used a technique that allowed me to turn those fears into a movie. I'd grab my popcorn and just watch them play out. Sometimes they had happy endings, sometimes they didn't. I tried distraction techniques, attempting to think of something else any time a worry popped up. This was somewhat useful, but like a young child who would rather play with the power drill than the toy train, my brain often returned to the worry as soon as I looked away. I even did yoga poses designed to release the fear from my body.

Overall, the traditional techniques were a flop, so I thought of a different approach: I'd give up worrying for Lent. Yes, that was a serious thought. I'd always been successful in my Lenten sacrifices, in part because I knew it had a bigger purpose. Why not give it a try? I knew it was going to be hard, but if I really could go forty days without worrying, how much happier would I be?

By the time I got out of bed the next morning, I'd already failed. But I wasn't ready to give up completely, so I kept trying. I resumed all the techniques I'd tried before, adding in prayer and hymns as a way of distraction. I also stepped up my mindfulness practices, noticing a thought and then letting it fade away without paying any attention to it.

All of it was a lot harder than I'd expected, even with God's help. I guess some habits are too hard to give up. Instead, I settled on a middle-ground solution. Though I knew I probably couldn't stop the worries, I didn't need to invite them in and fix them a meal. Not worrying was unrealistic, but not feeding those worries might be an achievable goal. So I changed my Lenten sacrifice. I decided I wouldn't Google anything for the rest of Lent. I could still use Google for things like finding a good restaurant, but I couldn't look up the restaurant's health inspection report. No Wikipedia for earthquake preparation. No election polling results and no checking the stock market. WebMD and all patient discussion boards were off limits.

At the end of the forty days, I felt less informed but a little calmer—a decent trade. Although the worries still came, I didn't make them worse. It was a start. Taming the noise in my brain was only the first step toward becoming fearless. I knew that the only way to truly stop being afraid was to do the things that scare me. It was time to take fear head-on and come running at it. I had to get out of my head and into the world.

Making Big Mistakes

I knew I couldn't just jump right into being adventurous. It had been a long time since I was bold and spontaneous. I didn't think my heart could handle jumping out of a plane or auditioning for a movie, so I started small. My first adventure was to go to the metaphysical fair (if you read the spirituality chapter, you can understand why this was kind of a big deal). I couldn't persuade any of my friends to join me, so I went by myself. I learned about my future, had my auras cleansed and got new crystals. I also learned that my spirit animal is a tortoise. Seems about right.

I did other things that would typically be considered scary. I held a tarantula at the zoo. I walked along the edge of the cliff of a local canyon and crossed the rickety bridge. I climbed the rock wall all the way to the top. I took a group of four-year-olds to see Christmas lights by myself. I went swimming in the public pool even though I hadn't shaved in several months. Bam—bold!

My next goal was to try to expand my diet. I didn't go all Bizarre Foods crazy, but I did try some new foods and enjoyed them, which gave me some hope. I even made it to a sushi place (but I didn't actually eat any sushi. One thing at time.)

As I took on these new adventures, I noticed myself becoming lighter. I was more joyful and it was easier not to take myself so seriously. It inspired me to do more. I figured that being bold would be more fun with a partner, so I tried to persuade my husband to join me in some new adventures. We had a hard time determining what we should do, though. This wasn't just about having fun. It had to be daring, so just going to a movie, even a really scary one, didn't count. We had to get outside our comfort zones. I suggested trapeze lessons. He didn't think we should hang upside down at our age. He suggested swing dancing. I called my insurance agent, who expressed concern about the safety of others based on my dance skills. He said our liability limits weren't high enough, so we said no, rather than take out a new policy. We finally settled on a cooking class. Although not really scary and bold, it is different from my regular routine. Just putting on real pants is bold for me. We haven't scheduled the class yet, but it is on our list. Look at that—I now have a bucket list.

I had another opportunity to try being bold. A neighbor had some tickets to a concert that she couldn't use and offered them to me. I came up with a hundred reasons not to go, but the band's songs played in my head all day. That must have been a sign that I should go, so I said yes. I didn't have anyone to go with me and I didn't have a babysitter yet, but I had the tickets!! Attending a concert may not seem like a very bold act, but it's actually a pretty big step for me. It was the first time in a long time (probably since my daughter's birth) that I planned to do something I wanted to do for no reason other than I wanted to do it. It had been a long time since I'd inconvenienced others so that I could do something I wanted to do. Bam—bold!

Unfortunately, the day of the concert I came down with a tummy bug. I gave the tickets to a friend, who had a fantastic time. I cuddled up in bed and fell asleep by eight. *Not* bold, but what are you gonna do? I forgave myself and got a good night's sleep.

Saying Yes

One of my goals in this experiment was to say yes more often. I'd been hiding behind "no" for too long. It was time to get back out there. I made the decision that I would say yes to anything that someone asked me to do. Anything. One friend invited me to a spiritual retreat and I went. We had to chant and throw things into a fire to let them go. I had a great time. Another friend invited me to a dance class and I went. I didn't fall down. I laughed and enjoyed the music. I'll probably even go back. My husband suggested that we go snowboarding. I fell down. A lot. My mother-in-law invited me to go to Seattle with her. Sure, why not? It was a great time. While no one suggested anything too crazy and I wasn't exactly pushed outside my comfort zone, it still felt nice to say yes to some tiny adventures.

Saying No

While I wanted to say yes to adventure, I didn't want to say yes to things that wouldn't serve me. I often have a hard time saying no. I sometimes have a hard time setting my limits and sticking to them. I can say no, but I'm also very easily persuaded. I don't know if this stems from guilt, from wanting to be helpful, from wanting to rescue others, or from believing that if I don't do it, no one will. Maybe it's just that inherent overachiever mentality that makes me think I have to take on everything that's presented. Regardless of the reason, I'm learning that agreeing to do everything doesn't serve me well. It creates obligations I don't want. Then I feel resentful about saying yes. Then I feel guilty for feeling resentful. Then I beat myself up and wonder if I'm a good person, a good friend, a good employee, etc., etc., etc. It's exhausting on so many levels.

As I learn more about happy people, I find that those who are the least stressed are also those with the best boundaries. They set limits on what they can do. They give themselves time and space, even if it inconveniences others. They say no.

While I said yes to adventure and new things, I said no to obligations and commitments. I turned down opportunities that I didn't think were right for me. I said no to taking on more than I could realistically do. I said yes to saying no. It was daring and bold. It was adventurous to let someone else do it. And I didn't even feel bad about it.

The Courage to be Happy

As I was working on this experiment and pondering being bold, I had a revelation. Happiness is bold. It takes courage to be happy. Worry, fear and anxiety are easy. I don't mean that living with anxiety is easy. Living with anxiety sucks. But getting worried, feeding those fears, and giving in to anxiety is easy. Anxiety, depression, sadness, worry, anger, and guilt will all show up when you least expect it and won't take the hint that they're not wanted. If you try to ignore them, they'll chase you down. They'll stand on your porch with chocolates and flowers. You may try to tell them, "Not today," but that won't stop them from showing up. Anxiety doesn't mind being a party crasher. It doesn't care what you think. It does what it wants.

But happiness is different. Happiness requires some courting. You have to make the first move. You have to woo it a little, persuade it to stick around. Then it may go away and you have to figure out how to win it back. Happiness is fickle. It will walk out the door at the first sign of trouble. You have to keep inviting happiness back in and making space for it to get comfortable.

This is where the courage comes in. It takes guts to court happiness and reject fear. It takes strength to try and be positive when it seems like the world around you is falling apart. It takes courage to keep looking for happiness when you're not even sure if it exists. It takes bravery to keep fighting fear to make room for happiness to come in. At times during my experiments, I wasn't sure if I had the courage to be happy. I wasn't sure if I was brave enough to not only take on new things but also to actively chase down happiness and fall deeply in love with it. I didn't know if I could tell fear, anxiety, sadness, and guilt "no." They can be pretty persuasive. I appreciate what they have to say, but it's not what I want in my life. I want to be happy. But it takes courage to choose happy rather than let the other emotions just take over. Fear, it's time I said good-bye to you. I'm not interested in what you have to offer. Happiness, how you doin'? Come on in.

Findings and Analysis

One of my favorite movies of all time is *What About Bob?* It's the story of a guy who follows his therapist on vacation. In the movie, Bob uses "the baby steps approach" to free himself of fear and anxiety, and I think that sums up this experiment. As much as I wanted to be bold and daring, I only took baby steps.

I tried to be bold. I did. I made a bucket list. Well, sort of. I came up with some ideas of things I'd like to do, and at some point, I will do that cooking class. I'd also like to run a 5K. I'd still like to see that concert I missed. And I still hope to get to Machu Picchu one day. One day. Until then, it's baby steps.

While this experiment reminded me of my adventurous and brave spirit, it also pointed out to me how often I do listen to fear. That isn't the life I want to live. I want to be brave. I want to be bold. I want to say yes to adventure. I hope to stop fear from running my life and ruining my fun. If I could tackle my fear, happiness would be so much easier. I have to keep practicing. I have to keep telling fear "no" to make space for happiness. I have to have the courage to be happy. I want more adventures. I can't wait to make some really big mistakes. As they say, bad decisions make the best stories.

Chapter 13

The Search for Happy People

Bonus Experiment: Find a Happy Person

Methods:

- Ask people if they're happy
- Find out what their secrets are

Happiness Quotient: *10/10*

Experiment Design:

As I was nearing the end of my study, I felt like I had not found happiness. Rather, I was pretty disheartened. Was all this work worth it? Though I'd found moments of joy, I definitely wasn't happy. I'd done all these experiments, but it felt like life kept getting harder. My experiments were no match for mid-life stress. My attempts to find joy couldn't compare to the weight of the world. All my work seemed to be leading nowhere.

Not only was I not happier, I was ready to give up. I wanted to call it quits. I didn't think I would ever find happiness. In fact, I didn't even think it existed. There was just too much pain in my life, too much pain in the world. Everything I was seeing in society, on the news, and in conversations with others led me to believe that everyone was miserable. But I wanted to make sure my own experiences weren't clouding my data. Being a good scientist, I determined that I would come up with a new experiment to test my theory before I scrapped everything.

Let me first clarify, this wasn't actually a scientific study or a formal research process. It was more like the philosopher Diogenes's search for an honest man. I was feeling hopeless and needed some reassurance that there was still happiness in the world. I needed a reason to keep trying. Unlike actual research studies that rely on multiple data points to confirm a theory, I was willing to take a single case scenario. I made the decision that if I could find even one person who could tell me that happiness is possible, I'd keep going. So I went on a slightly different search for happiness.

I started by just asking people who were older than me if life gets any easier, kind of like an It Gets Better Project for forty-year-olds. I wanted to chalk this whole thing up to a midlife crisis and believe that in a few years everything would feel fine. I asked people what the easiest and hardest times of their lives were, but no one would give me an answer. They all said things like, "There were struggles and happy times through each stage of life. They were all different. Different goals. Different problems. Different struggles. Different joys." I get it. Life isn't that simple. It's complicated at all ages. But that didn't help me. I guess I just wanted someone to tell me that at some point it gets easier. I just wanted some type of hope. Thanks for nothing, old people.

Since I didn't get the answer I was looking for, I didn't automatically assume happiness doesn't exist. I reevaluated my research design again and concluded that maybe I wasn't talking to the right people or asking the right questions. I chalked up the It Gets Better Project to sampling error and tried again. I no longer focused only on those who had a lot of life experience but decided to expand my sample to include everyone. *That* should solve my sampling error problem. I also revised my question. Although I personally wanted someone to tell me that things get easier, the point of my experiment was to determine whether happiness exists. Instead of asking people about their lives in general, I specifically asked if they were happy. Could I find even one happy person?

The answer was "yes." To my pleasant surprise, I found many. Although I still got the stock answer of how there are good times and bad times, people were able to say with some certainty that they're happy with their lives. These brave people provided some hope that happiness, life satisfaction, and contentment are possible, which is good news for all of us. But that wasn't enough. I also wanted to know why. What was it about their lives that made things so great? Could they somehow impart to me the secret of happiness? I certainly hoped so.

Methods

My methods of locating people were very unscientific. I started with Facebook because that's where all good collaborations start. I simply put up a post asking, "Are you happy?" This caused a lot of controversy. Some people replied, "Not at the moment," or, "I will be after the Super Bowl," or made other comments about temporary happiness. When I tried to clarify that I was asking about long-term happiness, this was met with more controversy, with people saying the emotion of happiness is not a constant. I agree. The old people had already told me that.

Happiness professor Javy Galindo offers this definition: "Happiness is more than a positive emotion. It is the state of a life well-lived." That's what I wanted to know. Was anyone leading a life well-lived? I revised the question and asked, "Are you someone who is overall happy with your life?" This seemed to be easier for people to understand.

I don't have many Facebook friends, especially when measured by digital standards, but of the two hundred or so friends I have, about ten responded. I sent them a list of five questions and asked them to send it back to me with answers. I used snowball sampling from there, asking my Facebook friends to pass it along to other happy people. I also began asking others I knew. I asked people at church, I asked at my library group, I asked at the playground while sitting with other moms. In fact, almost anywhere I went, I began talking with people about their happiness. They answered my questions but also connected me to others who might be happy. Suddenly, I had responses from lots of different people from lots of different walks of life.

In all, I gathered information from about sixty-five happy people. The ages ranged from twenty-six to ninety-seven. Most of the participants were women, but there were a few men who also contributed. There were varying races/ethnicities, socioeconomic statuses, occupations, religions, and life experiences. There were no specific criteria for people to participate other than self-reported happiness. Although my methods were primarily qualitative, I did ask each of them to take the Oxford Happiness Questionnaire so that I would have a basis for comparison for my own scores. The mean score was 4.58 (sd=.28), and according to the Oxford Happiness Questionnaire guide, anyone with a score over 4 is typically regarded as a happy person. As measured by this scale, these were happy people.

However, it wasn't their scores that convinced me. It was their stories. As I talked with people, I heard tales of true happiness. There were people who loved their lives. Although my sample was small and I can't be definitive, it appears as though happiness just might exist.

Findings and Analysis

Although my initial question was only if happiness existed, that wasn't enough for me. I also wanted to know why people were happy. After I'd heard a number of different stories, I began coding the responses to determine any patterns. I wanted to see if I could combine the stories from the happy people to magically uncover the secrets to happiness. I'm sorry to report that I *didn't* find the secret to happiness. I did find a few interesting things:

- **Some people are naturally happy.**

  There is a group of people who are naturally happy. They don't do anything to be happy, they just are. About 20% of my participants fell into this category. They report an overall contentment with their lives and report feeling happy or being in a good mood most of the time. While they have their struggles just like everyone else, they don't let the bad times get them down. When problems arise, they focus on solutions. If they can't solve the problems, they let them go.

Their secret is that they don't worry. They appear to have low levels of neuroticism (I'd have to do further testing to confirm this). Testing may not even be necessary as all of them acknowledge that they don't worry. What's more, most of them report that they've always been this way, even through really big problems and difficult situations.

What was most interesting to me is that they don't do anything specific to make their lives happy. They don't do anything to avoid problems. They roll with the punches and take things as they come. This isn't to say they don't have dreams or goals. They do. And they're excited about them. But they also live day by day and appreciate what they currently have. I often wish happiness were that simple, and for these people it is.

Most people have to work at happiness.

While it would be lovely to be one of those people who are naturally happy, most of the happy people reported having to work at it. There was a similar narrative among those people: Something crappy happens, they realize they aren't happy, and they make a conscious decision not only to change the circumstance but also to never go back to being unhappy again. Then they take steps to maintain that happiness.

There are many other commonalities among this group. For one, they have an awareness of their own feelings. They do regular "happiness check-ins" to evaluate how their lives are going. If they find something in their lives that isn't making them happy, they take steps to change it. Unlike the naturally happy group, this group feels emotions strongly, gets overwhelmed by problems, and has a tendency to worry and ruminate about things. However, because they've made a decision to be happy, they acknowledge what they're feeling, determine how to solve the problem, and then move on. The good news is that although they have to work at it, it gets easier over time. They don't have to work quite as hard as they once did.

The techniques they use to manage their stress and make themselves happy vary from person to person, but all of them report doing regular activities to increase their levels of happiness. The common activities include regular self-care routines, like getting nails done or treating themselves to coffee. Time with friends and family is very important, and gratitude was cited as a regular practice for staying happy. Volunteering or caring for others in some way was reported as something that routinely brought about happiness as well. Some report finding happiness in their jobs or achievements. Some also report using specific techniques aimed at managing anxiety, like going to therapy, practicing meditation, and journaling. These people also sought happiness and found it. It appears that not only does happiness exist, but if it's missing, you can do things to get it. Very good news for all of us.

Regardless of whether happiness came naturally or whether people worked at it, there were some commonalities of the lives of happy people[6]:

- Relationships. Every single person who reported that their life was happy also reported that they had good relationships. Many of them reported that spending time with family and friends is what made them happy. Many of them reported relying on friends and family in tough times. Many of them also cited their families as their greatest joy and losing family as their greatest fear. Every happy person reported having important people around them. I don't think this is a coincidence.

- Spirituality. Across both groups, believing in a higher power or trusting the universe was routinely cited as a source of happiness or calm. Prayer, talking to dead relatives, or even just believing that the universe would help them was the source of happiness. Many people felt as though they didn't need to worry because God or the universe or whoever would help them. However, religion itself was a mixed bag in terms of happiness.

  Some reported finding happiness through their church partici-

6 I just want to clarify that these are only commonalities, not causes. Many people who *aren't* happy also have good relationships, spirituality, boundaries, etc. My current research design isn't strong enough to definitively determine any causes of happiness. (That's what you get for using qualitative methods, am I right, my quantitative peeps?) At any rate, my next book uses a more scientific, two-group comparison design to sort some of this out. You'll just have to wait until then for any real answers.

pation, but many reported that formalized religion, religious expectations, and religious guilt were sources of great unhappiness. In theses cases, the happy people engage in spiritual practices but don't necessarily participate in formalized religion.

- Boundaries. Happy people say no. While they reported gaining a lot of joy from helping others, they're aware of the need to care for themselves, too. They don't overwhelm themselves with the problems of others. They have a good awareness of their own limits and are willing to respect those limits.

- Resilience. It might be easy to believe that these people are happy because nothing terrible has happened to them. Or maybe they just don't know how messed up the world is. But that isn't true. Almost all the participants had been through loss, betrayal, grief, or some type of serious life-changing event. And they all recovered from it. Many of them reported growing as a result, learning a lesson from it or, in many cases, using horrible events as the catalyst for becoming happy. All of them reported being able to move past these events. They don't live there anymore. They are resilient.

- A belief that things will work out. They trust that everything is going to be okay. They look at life's challenges and have faith that they can get through whatever may happen. I'm not talking about optimism or trying to be positive. In fact, some of the happy people were quite negative and complainy. Rather, it is a bigger picture notion that everything falls into place as it should. They can see the light at the end of the tunnel. They don't just hope things will work out. They know it.

- Living one's passion or finding meaning. For many people, when they felt as though they were making a difference in the world, they felt happy. Some got this from their careers, some from raising families, some from organizations or community activities. Regardless of where they found meaning, when they felt like they were doing something useful and contributing to society, they found happiness. They felt like they were doing what they were "supposed" to be doing.

It gets better. As I initially suspected, there is a developmental process to all this. While the old people didn't really help me to know when I would find happiness, there were some commonalities among different periods of their lives, patterns in the timing of happiness. For many, the early adult stage was happy. Life was new and full of possibilities. While there were a lot of stressors, there was also a lot of hope. The respondents routinely reported "midlife" as the most challenging. Starting families, being fully engaged in career, work stresses, financial stresses, and family stresses were all cited as things that made midlife less happy. In a related finding, older respondents said retirement was their happiest time. They report having freedom to explore who they were and what they wanted to do. They also report that by about age sixty, they stopped worrying about whether they were happy. They just enjoyed where they were and what they had. This appears to be the time of relaxation and gratitude, both key factors in happiness. My recommendation for those who don't want to work at happiness is just wait. With any luck, by about age sixty it will all make sense.

Conclusions

Although my goal was to find a happy person, doing this research brought *me* a lot of happiness. I enjoyed talking with people. I enjoyed hearing their stories. I was reassured by their resilience and confidence. Looking for happiness in others brought me happiness. What a serendipitous finding.

As for the happy-people findings, I don't really know what any of this means. Mine isn't the first study about happiness, nor will it be the last. There have been many others. And I don't think I found anything groundbreaking. Most of what these people report is already noted in the literature. But, expanding the happiness literature wasn't the point of this study. The reason for me to ask people about happiness was self-serving and personal. It was a way to provide me with hope. I needed to know that it was worth it to keep trying. I needed to know that everything I was doing would eventually pay off. I wanted to know that things get easier. I needed to know that happiness is possible and that it exists. These happy people gave me what I needed: the strength to keep looking. Happiness is out there. Thank you, happy people. Thank you.

Chapter 14

The Transformation

Area of Inquiry: Do nothing

Methods:

- Let go of the things that are getting in the way of my happiness
- Implement the things that make me happy
- Let happiness find me
- Wait

Happiness Quotient: 9/10

Experiment Design:

Although I had been working really hard on these experiments, I felt like it wasn't really making any difference. I had found some fun and moments of happy, but I didn't seem to be finding what I was looking for. As the winter months approached and the weather turned gray, my mood followed. It wasn't just a bad mood, I felt as if I'd reached a place of darkness. I wasn't happy. In fact, I didn't even believe happiness was possible anymore. I'd been through a lot: my husband's job change, the removal of my kidney stone, my mother's health issues, job stress, my child's multiple ear infections, and trying to not get sucked into the collective emotions of a very angry and divided post-election country. I know that it is common for people to run into obstacles on their quests, but I felt like this was all too much. How on earth was I going to find happiness when I could barely get through the day?

In the happily ever after stories, the heroes often become tired and want to give up the quest. The same was true for me. I realized how exhausted my body and mind were. I knew something needed to change. A visit to the playground, talking with a friend, and my morning meditations brought momentary relief, but this was bigger. Life was just too damn hard. I needed answers, but I wasn't even sure what the questions were. I just knew my life wasn't working, regardless of how hard I was trying to be happy. I was doing all the things that "should" make me happy, so why was I still so miserable? I didn't know, but I needed to find out. My sanity depended on it.

When researchers are committed to their content but their experiments aren't working out, they revise their design. Maybe I didn't need to give up completely; maybe I just needed to adjust my plan. Chasing happiness wasn't bringing it any closer. I went back to the literature to see if I could figure out what happens when people get stuck in their searches for happiness. I came across a book called *When the Heart Waits*, by Sue Monk Kidd, in which she writes about her midlife crisis. She navigated through it by doing nothing. She sat in the darkness of her life and waited. She decided to stop trying so hard and simply waited to see what God had planned for her. She likened the crisis to a cocoon, a dark place for growth and transformation to occur. It was a novel approach and different from everything else I'd been doing. Maybe I was just working too hard. Maybe I needed to stop searching for happiness. Maybe I needed a rest. Maybe I needed to do nothing.

So that's what I did. For my final experiment, I decided that I wouldn't do anything. I would build my cocoon around me, sit in the darkness, and patiently wait. I would wait for the answers. I would wait for the questions. I would give myself time and space to transform and grow. I would wait for happiness to find me. And that's exactly what happened.

Making Space

Once I had made up my mind to put my experiments on pause, I decided to spend my days just reading, thinking, and waiting. It seemed like a perfect plan for a cocoon. But in the first week of my official cocooning, I had something scheduled for every single day. I had doctors' appointments, church meetings, and parties at my daughter's school. In addition, although I'd officially quit my job, I was still working for the company on a contract basis to complete some lingering projects. For someone who was doing nothing, I was certainly doing a lot.

My attempts to cocoon weren't working. I was just too busy to do nothing. When I thought about why I was so busy, I realized that I was doing the exact same things that I had always done, following the same patterns that had brought me to this place of darkness. I needed a better plan. I had to do something different. I had to make some decisions. While looking at my schedule, I came to the conclusion that if I have only so much to give, I need to give it to the things that matter. I had to focus on what was important. Unfortunately, I wasn't even sure what that was. My head and my heart weren't clear enough for me to know what to prioritize. Instead of making any decisions, I dumped it all. I got rid of everything I could. I dropped all commitments and obligations. I even got rid of the things I knew would likely bring happiness, like volunteering. I still did laundry and paid bills, picked up my daughter from school and put her to bed at night, and responded to my e-mails and texts (most of the time), but I began saying no to everything else. Eventually my calendar was empty. There was no place I had to be but alone with my thoughts.

The Remodel

My first experiment in this happiness project was to get my space organized. I had to prioritize what I was going to keep and what I was going to let go. I had to decide what objects were worthy of the limited space in my house. I realized I needed to do the same for my life. Once I was alone with my thoughts, I learned how much space all those thoughts occupied. There were a lot of useless things taking up valuable real estate in my head and I needed to clean house.

Through some of my experiments, I was able to trade in many of those useless thoughts for something better. I let go of things holding me back to make room for new things. I let go of an angry God to make room for grace. I let go of thinking I could never be vulnerable, which allowed me to receive help from my tribe. I let go of fear and replaced it with being bold. I let go of taking myself too seriously so I could have fun. But that wasn't enough.

Although I had freed myself from commitments and had already let go of some false beliefs, my cocoon still seemed really crowded. What was it that was still getting in my way? Until now, I'd only been scratching the surface of happiness. Though these experiments created periods of joy, I felt like I was missing something bigger. Then I realized that I had some things in my life that I'd been ignoring, just like my bathroom from the first experiment. There were things deep in my core that needed reorganization. It was time for an identity remodel.

Who I'm Supposed to Be

Over the past few years, I've undergone some pretty big changes in my identity. I've always known who I was and what I wanted from life. I've always found it easy to be me, and I lived my authentic self every single day. But with everything that had happened over the last few years, I realized that I didn't really know who I was anymore. I became a parent, which changed my roles, my daily activities, my relationships, and my priorities. I reached a milestone in my education, not realizing that this would so significantly affect my career choices. I'd taken on the adventures of parenting and getting my degree because I thought they would make me happy, but these changes just ended up making me question who I was. I didn't feel happy, I just felt lost.

Since I didn't know who I was, I listened to others' ideas of what my life should be. I let other people tell me what was important. I'd never been a parent or an academic before. I didn't know what to do or how I was supposed to feel. I figured others knew better than I did. And I tried really hard to make myself want all the things that were "supposed to" make me happy. I thought I could talk myself into being happy. But as Grandpa Troll says in *Frozen*, "Hearts are not that easily persuaded."

Although I had taken on each of these challenges willingly, I didn't think about how they would change me (my authentic self is pretty impulsive). I don't regret my choices and I'm not going to give my child or my degree back, but I needed to grow into my new roles and understand how they had affected my identity and, ultimately, my happiness. I decided I would use my time in the cocoon to sort it out. That's what cocoons are for, right?

#sorrynotsorry

After my daughter was born, I didn't have any idea what I was doing. Luckily for me, everyone in the world seems to have an opinion on parenting. Why are you giving your child Cheetos for breakfast? Don't you think it's too cold for her to be wearing a short-sleeved shirt? Shouldn't you be using natural organic sunscreen? Why are you letting her play with the band saw? Everyone had something to say. I was trying my best to show others that I could be a good mom, but it was never really about the child care. I knew how to warm up strained peas and give her a bath. I didn't know how to be a mom. I didn't know how moms navigated their lives. I didn't know how moms found happiness. I didn't know how to be a mom and still be the same person I was before. And when I got sick, I lost what little confidence I had because I didn't know how I was supposed to take care of both of us at the same time. I just wanted to be me again and I wasn't sure how to do that with a child by my side.

Most people in my life figured that I would never be a mom. It wasn't because I wasn't nurturing or kind—it just didn't fit the picture of me that they had in their heads. I don't know why, but according to many of my friends and colleagues, they never saw me as the "mom type."

I guess I believed them and never figured myself to be the mom type either. Maybe this is why I found becoming a parent so hard. I felt like I was sacrificing a lot to parent her. Not only was I sacrificing my career, my sleep, my friendships, and my free time, but also my sense of humor, and my cool, independent, feminist, free-spirit personality. As much as I loved being with my daughter and being a parent, I didn't know how to be a mom and a cool, independent, feminist, free spirit. Could I be both?

In short, the answer is "no." Being a parent changes you. I couldn't just be the same person I was before. My time in the cocoon taught me that was okay because I could be something else. That's what happens in a cocoon—the caterpillar becomes something new. Maybe I didn't have to remain an ambivalent and hesitant mom longing for my care-free days. Instead of trying to fit myself into a mold of who others thought I was, I decided to redefine myself and create a new "mom type."

I can't really say how this happened, other than that I simply accepted that I was a parent. I'd spent a lot of time thinking about how I'd traded my independence for anxiety, which isn't really a very fair trade. However, there were other things gained in this trade that I was forgetting about: love, hope, and a reason to be happy. When I could appreciate this, I stopped lamenting all I'd lost and switched my focus to all I'd gained from having my daughter in my life. Suddenly, I had a lot of gratitude for her and all the ways in which she's helped me grow, all the ways she helps me to be happy. She's a big part of everything I do. I'm no longer independent and my spirit isn't quite as free, but I am a feminist and pretty darn cool. I'm not the same person I was before I had her. I'm better. I'm still me, just a happier, stronger, more patient, more compassionate, more grown-up version of me. I didn't need to find a way to fit into some outdated societal definition of a mom. I could create my own.

Once I was able to accept myself as a mom, I found it to be a lot easier to let go of what others thought of me. I didn't care if people agreed with my parenting choices. I didn't need to live up to anyone's expectations of who they thought I was or who I should be. I didn't need anyone to tell me how to be a mom. We were doing just fine. I love being her mom and parenting is something I want in my life, but that doesn't mean I have to completely give up all aspects of my old self. I can be whatever I want to be, even if I have a child. I do know how to be a mom and I trust myself with that—finally. I know others may question my choices, but I don't care. Most likely, my daughter will still wear short sleeves on cold days, have Cheetos for breakfast, and she'll probably never have organic sunscreen.[7] And I'm not even the littlest bit sorry about it.

---

7 But she can't use the band saw. Everyone knows a table saw is more efficient for toddlers.

While pretty much everyone was surprised that I'd become a mom, almost no one was surprised that I was going to get my PhD. *That* sounded like something I would do. I like education and I like intellectual pursuits. Unlike many of my classmates, I didn't go into the program with any expectations about what this would mean. I was actually just looking for something to provide amusement in my free time. Some people take up painting, some take dance lessons, but me, I figured I'd get a doctorate.

However, after I graduated, I didn't know what I was supposed to be doing. Apparently, with my new set of skills and a bunch of letters behind my name, I was expected to find a faculty position at some prestigious university where I would live the dream of achieving tenure. Yes, it was a lot of work, but it was the dream. The collective dream. But I didn't know how to be an academic, so I listened to others. I applied for faculty positions I didn't want. I wrote academic papers that were uninspired. I conducted research for others that was not important to me. I attended conferences for no reason other than the free happy hour appetizers and the off chance I might get to see some semi-famous researcher singing drunk karaoke. For about three years, I tried to be that academic everyone expected me to be. Even my job at the research firm was primarily to show others they hadn't wasted their time educating me. I didn't want to let my mentors and advisers down. But it seemed like I wasn't going anywhere with it. Interviews never seemed to work out, papers got rejected, and I just seemed to lose interest. Like Katy Perry says, "Maybe there's a reason why all the doors are closed." I began to wonder if this was the life intended for me. I was tired of navigating the politics of the ivory tower. I hated to say it, but I really didn't want to be a PhD anymore.

In my cocoon, I realized I could be something new. I didn't have to be anything that didn't fit me. I could be whatever I wanted, regardless of what letters were behind my name. I could go back to being a therapist. Or I could work at Target. Or I could be a stay-at-home mom. Or I could use the skills for something else (like studying happiness). My degree and years of study didn't have to define me. The more I thought about it, I don't know if it was that I didn't want to be an academic or if I was just tired of letting a job be my only source of pride and inspiration. I came to realize that I really didn't want my business card to be the most important thing about me. So I let it go. No more research or faculty job searches. No more journal manuscripts. No more grant applications. While I may conduct the occasional statistical analysis just for fun, I don't think an academic or research job is for me, at least not right now. It feels good to finally say that. Despite the fact that there were a lot of people who were invested in my education and future prospects, I don't feel sorry for straying from the tenure track. Not sorry at all.

Free to Be Me

In reality, maybe no one expected me to be a perfect mom or a great academic. Most people probably didn't feel strongly about what I should do. But whatever the truth was, I was tired of feeling like I was living someone else's life. I felt like the more I tried to be the person I assumed other people thought I was, the more lost I got. I don't think this is unusual. I think many of us lose our happiness in the expectations of others. But others can't make us happy. We have to live the lives meant for us, regardless of what anyone else thinks. Once I decided to follow my own path and let go of others' expectations, I found the space I needed to be me and the strength I needed to continue my quest. I suddenly felt as if a weight had lifted.

During my time in the cocoon, I had actively let go of obligations, commitments, time constraints, false beliefs, and unrealistic expectations. I discarded all the things that were keeping me from living a happy life. I eliminated the things weighing me down. I finally had all this space to breathe, space to grow. I could finally take the final step in my journey and transform. But how was I going to make that happen? Oddly, the answer was to continue to do nothing.

Analyzing the Data

In research, once all the data is collected, there's a period of inactivity. The researcher needs a chance to sit with the data, to play with it, to wrestle it and massage it. I'd collected a year's worth of data about happiness, and I had a pretty good idea about what made me happy. From my time in the cocoon, I also had a pretty good idea about what made me unhappy. Now I just needed to pull all my findings together and make recommendations about how to live a happy life. But I had no idea what recommendation to make. I didn't have an answer, so I let the data sit, hoping something would reveal itself eventually.

I wanted to escape my quiet desperation, but I didn't want to jump into something else that would just make me miserable. So, taking my own advice, I did nothing. I felt better about having decided what I want from life, but I didn't do anything with it, at least not right away. I didn't work at happiness, I just lived the life that was right in front of me. I didn't fill up my time or continue to search for some new secret of happiness I may have overlooked. I just went about my day-to-day and took things as they came. I did what I wanted to do, like volunteering and playing with my child. I said no to things I didn't want to do. I just let myself be for a little bit. Slowly and without warning, happiness began to work its way in. Every day, I noticed myself laughing, smiling, and joking more. I worried less and found that it was easier for me to be present with whatever I was doing at the time. I felt calm. I felt happy. I felt peace. In some strange twist, doing nothing made me feel happier with my life than I had in a long time.

Once I got out of the way, a lot happened. All the work I'd done over the course of the year turned out to be more than looking for happiness. I wasn't just experimenting with adding things in and letting things go, I was incorporating them into my being. It's kind of like the caterpillar who eats everything in sight before entering the cocoon. He needs all that nourishment to sustain the cocoon to ultimately transform. The same was true for me. I needed all of my previous happiness experiments to carry me through the hard parts of growing. Once I actually gave myself time and space to let my experiments transform me, beauty began to emerge. Without my doing anything, opportunities began to present themselves. I only had to decide whether to accept their invitations.

As I began to write down final thoughts about the project, I recognized that writing my story had made me happy. The process of writing suits me well, and I've come to love writing. It feels like a natural part of identity, a comfortable part. And though I started writing as a way to heal, I began to wonder if others might benefit from my story. I didn't set out to write a book, but within a few weeks, things began happening without really trying. I found out that a friend of a friend is a book designer. A person I met at a party knew an editor. A friend who's an author reached out to me to offer advice. I liked the idea of being an author, and I guess the universe did, too.

I also found happiness in talking about happiness. As I began to tell others about my experiments, I was surprised by how much people wanted to know more about this topic. I was offered opportunities to study and talk about happiness even further. I was asked to review a journal article evaluating a program teaching happiness to children. Look at that—I was now officially a happiness researcher. A friend started her own happiness project and asked me for help on it. Suddenly, I was a happiness consultant. People continued to ask me about happiness and asked for suggestions about adding happiness into their lives. I guess that made me a happiness expert.

Although I wasn't looking for employment, a former co-worker and friend asked if I'd like to do some consulting. He connected me with some people who were looking for someone to do some mental health work. I told them about my happiness experiments and they were intrigued. They invited me to come join them to help people find happiness. I'm now getting paid to talk about happiness. But I only work part time so that I can go to the park with my child, volunteer, see my friends, and leave myself plenty of time to do nothing. That all makes me really happy.

As all of this started to unfold, though, I wasn't sure if I was ready. I didn't know if I had the courage to accept these invitations for happiness. I wasn't sure if I was ready to take on anything new. I was pretty comfortable with my cocoon. I liked doing nothing. But I also really liked writing and talking about happiness. As I was sitting on the porch pondering what to do, I looked down and saw something stuck to my sock. It was an empty cocoon. It was a pretty clear sign from God that I was ready.

Findings and Analysis

Of all the experiments, this one was the most important. It's where I should have started. I just didn't know that at the time. When I decided that I wanted to be happier, I let others tell me how to do it. I read the research and relied on the experts. I trusted friends, family, bosses, therapists, preachers, and mentors. I listened to society. I tried to emulate happy people. Even taking on this project was Gretchen Rubin's idea, not mine. I figured others knew better than me how to find happiness. I did what they said. I did all of it. I worked really hard at happiness. But it didn't make me happy.

In some weird paradox, it wasn't until I stopped doing everything that I was able to find happiness. Like with the first experiment in cleaning out my house, I had to let go of a lot of things. I had to let go of obligations and commitments. I had to let go of fears and regrets. I had to let go of who others thought I was. I had to decide for myself who I was and what would make me happy. Once I removed the clutter that was making me unhappy, I could choose what I wanted to keep. I kept the things that made me happy. I didn't need to continue to fill up my life with doing more. I did less. I gave my time only to the things I cared about. With my extra time, I was able to just be, exist, and be present with all that life has to offer. And that's where I found happy.

I came across this quote the other day: "The ego says, when everything is in place, I will find peace. The Spirit says, when I find peace, everything will fall into place." I now realize the Spirit is right. I was putting all these things into my life hoping to create peace. I couldn't find peace because I was working too hard. Once I slowed down, did less, and took the pressure off myself, I finally found some peace. And when I began living my life based on who I was and what I wanted, everything else fell into place. Including happiness.

Summary, Conclusions, and the Final Analysis

As I talk about my work, a lot of people ask me if I know the secret to happiness. After all the reading, all my interviews with happy people, and all my experiments, I can say with great certainty that I don't know. I don't know that I can sum up happiness from my experiments. Each individual experiment had some positive findings. Each of the experiments helped me to grow in some way. I had some difficulties, but I also had a lot of fun. The project itself sustained me through some of the tough times and gave me hope.

Gretchen Rubin suggests that we need to make only small changes to achieve happiness. For me, it required a life overhaul, a complete remodel. I did need to examine some of the small things and day-to-day activities that bring me joy, but that wasn't enough. I also needed to go deeper to examine my core beliefs, values, and identity. When I started this project, I just wanted to feel better, but I guess the universe had more in mind.

I like to blame all my unhappiness on getting sick, but that wasn't really the tragedy. Yes, getting sick stole my confidence and heightened my fears, but the illness was really just a symptom of something bigger. I realized that I'd stopped paying attention to my life. I forgot who I was and what was important. That was the real tragedy. Getting sick was merely the wake-up call, reminding me that I don't want life to just happen to me, I want to be an active part of it. I want to be true to who I am and live those values each day.

By experimenting with happiness, I was able to remember the things that I value and make me happy: having fun, serving my community, being with others, caring for my child, and my relationship with God. I also found the things that didn't make me happy: giving my time to things I don't care about, trying to live up to other people's expectations, outdated social definitions, and trying to "do it all." While the current happiness authors suggest that we need to add things into our lives and take active steps toward increasing our happiness, they don't talk much about eliminating the things that distract from our happiness. I didn't need to add more in—I needed to take things away. Once I eliminated the things weighing me down, happiness found its way in. The less I did, the happier I became. In an odd twist, I found happiness through subtraction.

I often wonder if this is a fallacy of the current thinking about happiness. We've been programmed to think that we need more and that if we can just work harder or do more, we'll find happiness. But based on my experience, I don't think it is about doing more. I think it's about doing the right things and doing less of the things we don't care about. Over the course of this project, I came to realize that I have limited time and energy and that I should devote it to the things that actually matter. I got rid of the things I didn't care about to make space for the things that did. When I began doing less, I found the time and energy to do the things I wanted to do. And I found a surprise. When I wasn't working so hard, I had time to just be. I was able to relax and enjoy the fruits of my labors, including happiness.

I recognize that things may not always be this way. There will be other challenges and difficult times. Although I'm content with my life, I still have worries, bad moods, and hard days. It's not as if once we're happy, we're happy every day forever. That would be nice, but it's not realistic.

Happiness and unhappiness can exist at the same time. We just have to learn to see the forest instead of the trees. We can have both a bad day and a happy life. I think people forget that. I know I did (and still do sometimes). But I'd like to think I learned some lessons through this process that will help me with the inevitable dark clouds. I don't want to think about that now so instead, I'll just appreciate the peace and simplicity I have in my life now and say, "Isn't this nice?"

Afterword

Happily Ever After

Some days, I'm not really sure this is my life. I honestly can't believe the transformation that's occurred. Once I got rid of the things I didn't want, there was plenty of space for the things I did want. And they came. Someone once told me that happiness is like a butterfly: If we chase it, it will fly away, but if we sit very still, it may just land on us when we least expect it.

Over the course of this year, I was creating the life I believe God intended for me. I just didn't know it at the time. I thought it took work to create happiness. It did. There was struggle. There was pain. There was work. But oddly, things got a lot easier for me when I stopped working so hard. At some point, I needed to just let happiness do its thing. I had to get out of God's way, let the Spirit work in my heart, and be grateful for the gifts offered to me. Today, I am grateful. I am so grateful.

The other day, I was doing some chores and watching my daughter play when a very calm feeling came over me. Things felt familiar. I felt like I'd come home. Now I can say that for the first time in a long time,

I believe I'm exactly where I'm supposed to be, doing exactly what I'm supposed to do. This is my life and it feels happy. I feel like my life reflects what's in my heart. I feel lighter. I feel like myself again. I finally found my awesome. Which is how happily ever after stories are written.

About the Author

Amy Lopez is an author, a happiness researcher, a clinical social worker, and a mom. She was born and raised in a small mountain town, spending most of her childhood on the ski mountain. She moved to the city to pursue her education, attending college at Regis University, and then went on to receive both her Master's in Social Work and her PhD in Social Work from the University of Denver. She has been a practicing social worker in mental health, child welfare, and the juvenile justice system. She currently works as a researcher and therapist, continuing to study happiness and help others find their happy. She is married, has one child, and lives in Colorado.

Works Cited

Argyle, M. & Hills, P. (2002). The Oxford happiness questionnaire: a compact scale for the measurement of psychological well-being. *Journal of Personality and Individual Differences*, 33, 1073-1082.

Galindo, J. (2013). *Authentic Happiness in Seven Emails.* Los Altos, CA: Hyena Press.

Gilbert, E. (2006). *Eat, Pray, Love.* New York: Riverhead Books.

Harris, D. (2014). *10% Happier*. New York: Harper Collins.

James. E.L. (2011). *Fifty Shades of Grey*. New York: Vintage Books.

Kabat-Zinn, J. (2013). *Full Catastrophe Living: Using the Wisdom of Your Body and Mind to Face Stress, Pain, and Illness (Revised Edition).* New York: Bantam Books.

Kidd. S.M. (2006). *When the Heart Waits: Spiritual Direction for Life's Sacred Questions.* (Revised Edition). New York: Harper Collins.

Moore, C. (2002). *Lamb: The Gospel According to Biff, Christ's Childhood Pal.* New York: Harper Collins.

Norris, K. (1996). *The Cloister Walk.* New York: Riverhead Books.

Strayed, C. (2012). *Wild.* New York: Vintage Books.

Rubin, G. (2009). *The Happiness Project: Or, Why I Spent a Year Trying to Sing in the Morning, Clean My Closets, Fight Right, Read Aristotle, and Generally Have More Fun*. New York: Harper Collins.

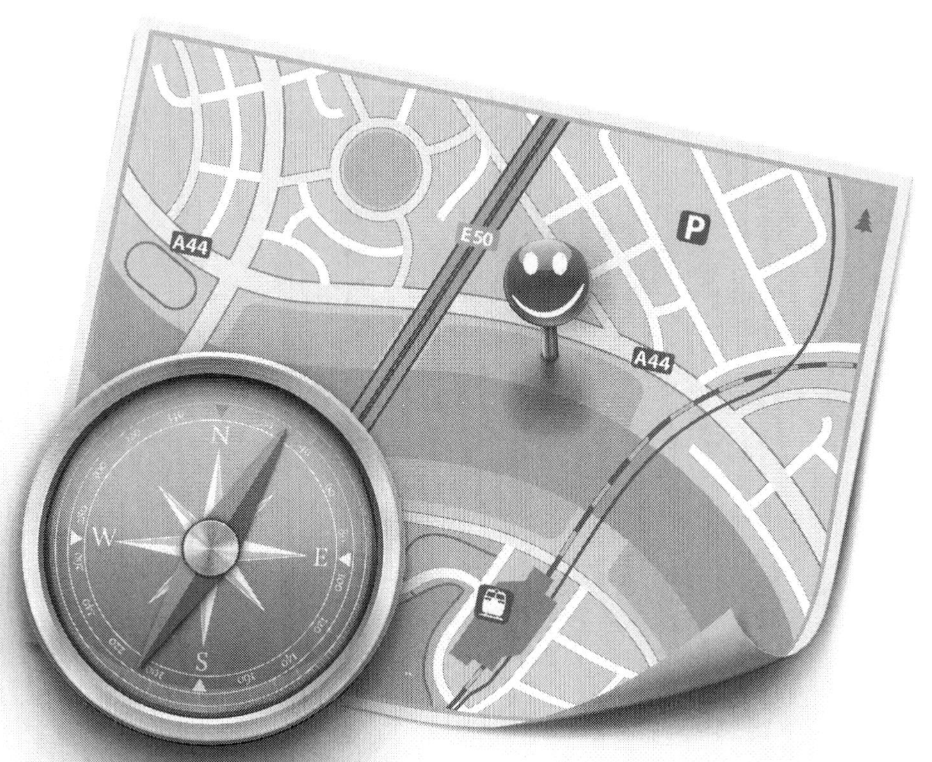

Want to try out the experiments for yourself? Check out our workbook to guide you through. It's a Choose Your Own Adventure Guide for navigating happiness. In the workbook, we provide exercises, ideas, and a road map to helping you find your own awesome. Coming soon. For more information, e-mail us at thesearchforawesome@gmail.com or thesearchforawesomeblog.wordpress.com.

Made in the USA
Columbia, SC
10 January 2018